Don't Give Up On Family Even if They're Furry

Why Your Dog's Bad Behavior is Your Fault

Candace D'Agnolo

Dedication

This book is dedicated to all the pets I've loved...
Smokey, Eve, Adam, Jenny, Prance (all cats by the way) and to
the dogs in my life Duke, Molly, Casey, Honey, Tyson, Guinness
& Clover. Especially Guinness & Clover for being there for me
during the tough times.

It's also dedicated to all the people I've loved...too many
to name...But I will say my mother, Karye Setterlund, always
inspired me to go after my dreams and supported my efforts
with Dogaholics in more ways than one. She also taught me the
word "that" usually isn't necessary and is always overused... so
now it's a huge pet peeve of mine. Hopefully, I haven't over
used it and my mom can be proud that my 'that's are in the
right place!

Contents

Bark Effectively: Communication and Creativity

Chase It Until You Catch It: Commitment and Consistency

When the Biscuit Crumbles: How to Roll with Setbacks

Every Dog Will Have Its Day

Preface

"Make the decision, then make the decision right." – Larry Winget

I hate to be the one to break it to you, but this book is not a dog training book. Maybe you picked it up hoping I would teach you all the tools you need to train *your dog* in minutes a day using barely any effort, but still achieving miraculous results. This book might be one of many you've flipped through looking for the solution to the dog issues that plague you, but it's the only book that will tell you the truth. Sit down for this one, it's a shocker.

Surprise! Your dog isn't the problem.

Yes, I'm going to help you work with your dog. I'm going to give you the tips and tools you need to make big changes in your pet parenting and your dog's life. I am going to help you *work with your dog,* but the biggest part of the process is *working on you.* No matter how many tricks I teach you, if you're not committed and motivated; if you're not ready to do the work and stick to it; if you don't know how having well-behaved dogs would make your life (and theirs!) better, then it doesn't matter. It won't work.

This book will help you understand how easy it is to fix any issue you are having with your pet whether behavioral or wellness related. Dogs *can learn* and *can change.* The first step – the step you must make before even starting the first chapter - is to stop making excuses that it's their fault they aren't behaving the way you'd like and acknowledge that it starts with you. (Stop making excuses for yourself, as well.) You may have heard that old dogs can't learn new tricks, but that's a big lie.

And frankly, you're the oldest dog in your house, so if you're willing to learn, you're in the right place.

This book will not only help you commit to your dog's training and find success, but it will open your eyes to other areas of your life that could use a little TLC and give you the tools to tackle them.

This book is not about puppy training techniques; it's not about canine nutrition; it's not about grooming or veterinary care. It also will not solve deeper behavioral issues in your pet relating to severe trauma. For those, consult an in-person trainer or behaviorist, but do your homework and choose a good one.

If you are feeling stress, anger, anxiety, or guilt because of your dog's behavior and you're ready to do something about it, then this book is for you. Perhaps you've tried training in the past and haven't seen results. Perhaps you feel like your dog has so many issues, you're overwhelmed by where to start. This book *will help you.*

This book is not for people who won't commit to being a responsible pet owner and who want to continue to enable their pet's bad behaviors. It is not for people who don't understand that their dog *wants to learn* and *wants to make them happy*. It is not for anyone looking for an excuse to relinquish their "problem" dog, nor is it for anyone who considers their pet more property than family.

Too many people are looking for quick fixes for their dog's bad behavior and health issues. I can tell you the quickest fix is by *you* committing to training and implementing simple techniques. When pet parents do this, they'll see positive results almost instantly.

I am the founder and owner of a retail and service business called Dogaholics with multiple locations, where since 2006, we've helped hundreds of thousands of dog owners make confident decisions about their pets' behavior and wellness through a curated selection of quality products, services and information.

Because of the transformations I've seen with my own dogs' behavior and many of my customers' experiences, I know all dogs can learn, no matter the age, breed or past life experience. I understand between your endless responsibilities, finding the time and motivation to train your dog isn't easy. Realizing your dog's behavior and actions is a direct reflection of who you are, as a pet parent, should become your motivation.

Owning a dog is a commitment. They are not a fad. They are not accessories. They are family. They should grow with you and change with you, because they are always loyal and committed to you.

CHAPTER ONE

Your Dog's Behavior is a Direct Reflection of You

*"The average dog has one request to all humankind.
Love me." –Helen Exley*

Bad dogs are the result of lazy owners. I know that sounds harsh, but hear me out.

Most of us are not living our best lives because of the lack of commitment we show to the decisions we've made. The lack of commitment (whether in the actions we take or the words we choose) has consequences that interfere with our health, our happiness, and our success. We don't achieve the good life, the extraordinary life, the life worth fighting for even though we all have an equal opportunity of obtaining it. Because of our lack of commitment to our decisions, the negative consequences of our decisions are often emotionally taxing, financially burdening or even truly life wasting. These consequences not only prevent us from living our best life but also interfere with the lives of those around us who we love and value—our kids, our spouses and yes, even our pets. The only way your life will change is if you change. I know it's possible; I've seen it happen in my own life and the lives of so many of our Dogaholics clientele.

If your dog is out of control, there's obviously something wrong with how you're interacting with that dog. Your dog's behavior is a direct reflection of you—your stress level, your commitment level, and your willingness to do the work of pet parent. The lesson that took me far too many years to learn is that if you're allowing your dog to behave that way, what else in your life is out of whack and chaotic? The dog's behavior can't be the only thing—we don't exist in a vacuum.

For that reason, as much as we want to change our dogs' behavior, this is a human training book. Just like in my business—while we sell products for dogs, the *dogaholic* is the *person*. The dogaholic is the one in the pet/human relationship who has all the control. The dogaholic, *you*, can commit to something better. Your basic dog training book might teach you how to be the alpha in your pack, and get your dog to shake and heel, but it stops there, and I'm here to tell you, if you stop there with it, you're missing out on an amazing and fulfilling life (with your dog).

How To Know You're In Chaos

The problem with chaos is we get so used to it, we don't even realize we're in it. You might be thinking, "My dogs aren't so out of control. They're just *dogs.*" You may be so busy managing everything you're presented with in your life, you don't even have time to notice it's unfulfilling.

The biggest, brightest, flashing neon sign alerting you to chaos is the feeling you're *missing out.* What *can't* you do right now—because of your dog, because of your job, because of your relationships, because of your finances?

For me, the catalyst was simple. I realized my lack of commitment to my own dogs was dictating my life—and it wasn't a life the dogs or I wanted to live.

We moved to a condo around the time when my two dogs, Guinness and Clover, were old enough to know better about their behaviors. My husband and I would go out to dinner and the woman who lived below us would send text messages to me complaining and asking when we were going to be home. Our dogs were being too loud and barky. I always felt horrible, not wanting her lifestyle to be disrupted because we were out having a good time. So, of course, we'd come home. We'd end our night early. We'd skip the movie or we'd take our dinner to go to avoid making her upset. Even when we did stay through dinner on a successful night out, I would constantly check my phone (don't you love that quality in a dinner companion?). I'd even call and check with her before making plans just to see if she was home.

My downstairs neighbor was in charge of my dinner plans, and she controlled my evenings out.

Did it occur to me I needed to find a way to control the barking, stop the separation issue, or stop the anxiety that was being created in the dogs? Or was it better to just *miss out*, because addressing the real issues would be too time-consuming, too inconvenient, or too *impossible*. I mean, they're just dogs, right? And they weren't puppies anymore.

It took me missing out on the dog park to realize something finally had to give. I owned a dog store, I *am* a dogaholic, and I couldn't go to the dog park with my dog. I live in a city with an amazing dog beach, and I wanted so badly to go, but I couldn't because Clover started dog fights. I asked myself, *why does she start dog fights?* Because she gets protective of me. Well, *why is she getting protective of me?* Because I tense up every time there's another dog around and she picks up on the tension. *What is the root of the problem?*

Me.

I'm tensing because *I'm nervous* she'll bite them. I realized if I didn't start working on myself I'd never be able to take her anywhere. I'd be missing out on something I want for *my life*. I want to be able to go to the dog beach with my dogs. It's a beautiful, fun place. I want to be able to go out to dinner without consulting the other houses on the block. I was missing out, and *I was the problem*.

Many of you have been nodding your head since the first chapter, but in case you're wondering *is this me*, here are a few ways to tell if you and your dog are taking a leash-walk through chaos.

Signs Your Dog Is Out Of Control:

- Excessive barking, or any extended barking when you're not home
- Jumps on people
- Lunges at other dogs
- Not walking in line with you or at least responsive to you (rather than up front or dragging behind on a leash walk)
- You can't have people over to your house because your dog is too protective, barks, or jumps
- You find yourself changing your life instead of being able to live it with your dog (changing plans, can't do things because of your dog)
- Neighbor – change your life instead of being able to live it with the dog
- If you don't know how to stop the jumping, barking, or unwanted behavior
- If your dog is overweight
- You're considering relinquishing your dog to the animal shelter or rehoming him

Signs Your Life Is Out Of Control:

- You're not paying your bills on time
- You can't get to work on time or you always want to leave early
- You're staying in a bad situation because it's easier than making a change or from a sense of duty
- You don't want to go see your family members
- You're afraid to make the changes you need in your life to be happy (it doesn't have to be monumental like a boss doing something illegal or marital infidelity. If it has to get to that sort of huge catalyst before you make a change, it's way too long to be suffering)

- You can't commit fully to what you're doing because you know it's not the right thing, but you haven't been willing to make a change to something else
- Your life is not bringing you joy

We only get one life, and we never know how long it's going to be. Our dogs' lives are even shorter. And the kicker? You are completely responsible for the quality of your dog's life from the time you have them until the time they die. You are *wholly responsible.* They can't get their own food, they can't get a job, they can't read, they can't turn on the television, they can't do anything without you. If you cannot commit to creating an amazing life for *yourself,* and if you can't choose to focus your energies on things that fulfil you, how do you expect to do it for your dog?

Chaos: Population Me

I've always prided myself on the fact I can handle a lot. Maybe you do, too. I mean, you have to be able to handle a lot because we have so much going on in this world. Our lifestyles are so scattered and busy—we're constantly running from one place to the next, from one thing to the next, and eternally connected while doing it.

I tell you this story not to frighten you, but to assure you chaos and I are old friends—and it's a friend I'm happy to have almost no contact with today.

When I had my startling realization *I was the problem I had been trying to solve*, I had three businesses in the dog market. Two of them could barely pay their bills, and my third one was making money, but having to pay the other two's way, leaving me with very little leftover. I had Guinness and Clover who were about a year or two old, we had just bought a great big house, and I was commuting from the suburbs – an hour into the city each way. We were in an unhappy marriage, and doing what lots of people do in unhappy marriages: we were trying to have kids.

My husband moved to New York, the recession hit, and though it was the plan for me to follow, I couldn't sell the business. Anyone who would have wanted to buy my business couldn't have gotten a loan. I owed money on a small business loan, and couldn't even walk away from it due to that obligation.

My business structure internally was totally chaotic and required my constant direct supervision, so there was no option to move to New York and just check in as needed. At the time, the plan was for me to follow in 6 months, spending the extra time getting the business in a position where I could.

Just after that, I found out an employee was embezzling money from me to the tune of about $40,000 — no wonder I couldn't pay the bills. It was then — slogging through this utter mess and trying to trust the team again I began wondering: *if this is happening – if I missed this – what else am I missing?*

I knew things had to change starting with me, but I had no idea how to make it happen. Even though I could barely pay my bills, I hired an expert. I wasn't taking a paycheck, myself, but I found a way to pay her. It seemed crazy at the time, but it worked. I had to really learn what wasn't working, and I had to regroup and start focusing on what *was* working and what *would* work.

I focused, chose to make the commitment back to the business, and found my motivation. I brought in an expert where I needed it to teach me the right way to run my store and most importantly get clarity on *exactly what I want* instead of just floating along.

You can't make a commitment to "whatever." It doesn't work.

I'm honored you've brought me in as your expert. This book will take you start to finish through the process of change—and you'll soon find your dog's behavior is progressing on par with your life—the one you have always wanted to live, rather than the one you were living by default.

Move through the book in order. Each set of exercises build from the last. Write in the book, and don't skip around (if you want to spoil the ending, I'll do it for you: your dog is suddenly listening to you, and your life is the one you thought you couldn't ever have).

In section one, I'll help you uncover why you have a lack of commitment and exactly how it happened. You'll be able to keep distractions and obstacles that block your goals at bay when you know what to watch for and how they trip you up.

In section two, you'll establish a new vision for yourself and connect with your motivation. You may not even realize you have options, and you may not know how to set about achieving them once you've chosen. It's okay, we'll work through it together.

Section three will give you the tools and strategies you need to live your best life and make your dog's life worthy of your dogaholic attributes. I'll show you how committing to your dog has repercussions in all areas, and how you can make small changes that have big impact.

Your dog is a family member, which is why you feel guilty when...

_____

_____

_____

_____

What one thing can you do today to move in a direction to release your guilt?

_____

_____

_____

_____

What activities do you want to do with your dog?

_____

_____

_____

_____

How would you like your dog to incorporate into your lifestyle?

_____

_____

_____

_____

What have you already taught your pet? What do you still need to teach?

_____

_____

_____

_____

How would your life look different if your dog listened to you?

_____

_____

_____

_____

Are you guilty of making other things a priority and forgetting about your dog? Explain it to yourself.

_____

_____

_____

_____

Where in your life do you see chaos occurring?

_____

_____

_____

_____

How have you tried to fix it? How successful were you?

_____

_____

_____

Pet Parent Bonding Activity

Go to your pet—Look him in the eyes and say, "I'm on the road to recovery. I'm not just going to be a dogaholic, I'm going to be a great pet parent!" Smile, and let him give you a kiss.

Now keep reading.

Part One:

Now You Stepped In It

Dogs Who Chase Their Tails Never Catch Anything

"Status quo, you know, is Latin for 'the mess we're in.'" –Ronald Reagan

You may never find yourself in a situation like mine with a business on the brink, short forty grand, and unable to even walk my dogs depending on the angle of the sun and how many people decided to come into the city that day. If you're not there (yet), congratulate yourself on figuring out you had a problem before the problem announced itself like an anvil to the head in an old Wile E. Coyote cartoon.

No matter how chaotic your situation is (or isn't), no matter how well you're coping with it, and no matter how many tips and tricks you try in your quest to fix it, you will *never* succeed at changing your dog's behavior or your own life unless you know *why* you got into the predicament in the first place.

You could buy all the anti-bark gadgets on the market, invent a few yourself like a mad scientist in your basement, and take wild, drastic measures, but unless you know why your dog is barking, he's not going to stop. If what you're doing now isn't working, there's a good chance you're being overly generous about the effort you've put in or you're focusing your effort in the wrong place.

It's funny when dogs chase their tails, right? Spinning around in a circle after the crazy wagging thing they can never quite catch. We can look at the spectacle with the kind of glee that only comes with seeing the big picture. When you're chasing after the solution to your problem—be it dog behavior or a life you aren't sure how you ended up with—without identifying the real heart of the problem, and thus knowing what a real solution would be, you look just like your dog. Except not quite so agile as you spin in the same endless circles.

Let's discuss the most common ways we invite the chaos both with our dogs and with our lives. When you do, you'll find the solution is a lot easier to come to (no spinning required).

CHAPTER TWO

How Did I Find Myself Here?
The Commitment Traps

"Life is really simple, but we insist on making it complicated." –
Confucius

If I had to pinpoint one thing as the genesis of most of
the chaos we bring upon ourselves, it would be our tendency to
say YES too often. Whether we want to please, whether we
want immediate gratification, whether we are conditioned to be
eternally helpful, we are saying yes at an alarming rate, and
we've turned NO into almost a curse word. I'm here to tell you
that "no" is not a curse. "No" is a blessing.

For me, it's always been a problem in my life because my
personality combines people-pleaser with superwoman. I feel
like I can take everything on, I can handle an enormous amount
of stress and things on my plate, and I keep adding more when
asked. And if this is you, you know they *always* ask, because
they know you will always say yes. And you, not wanting to miss
an opportunity, say yes even when you *know* you should say *no*.

I've grouped the four commitment traps in this chapter
together because they're all intertwined. Each one almost never
comes alone; it frequently brings a friend...or two...or three.
And these traps are equal opportunity offenders—your dog,
your relationship with your dog, and your own life are all fair
game.

Shiny Object Syndrome

As a culture, we are *constantly* distracted. Our attention
spans when measured in scientific studies average 4-6 seconds.

Most of us can't take two breaths without a distraction popping up – our phone goes off, email comes through, someone walks in, we're visual creatures and we notice something else. In today's world it is all but impossible to remain focused without vigilant effort.

Enter the shiny object. It's the thing we think we need. It's what distracts us from the uncomfortable, the difficult, the boring. If you're anything like me, your dog may even have been a living, breathing shiny object.

When Guinness and Clover came into my life, I was married to my ex-husband, Jimmy. We had a dog together named Tyson (you'll meet him later), and we loved Tyson. To be honest, I think I loved Tyson more than I loved Jimmy. Tyson grew ill later in his life and we had to put him to sleep. I've never grieved like I grieved for that dog. It was horrible.

Shiny objects distract us from hard things – they distract us from our commitment to things that are difficult to achieve (as we suffer through delayed gratification), from grief, sadness, pain, and struggle.

I serve on the board of Chicago Canine Rescue, and about three months after we put Tyson to sleep, a fellow board member reached out to me. She said, "Candace, there was a litter of puppies who had just showed up at the shelter and they just happened to name them all Irish names. So it's a sign! "

I was about to head off to Italy for three weeks, and I knew I was not ready for puppies. I had a fleeting thought of waiting until I got back, but those shiny objects glitter just in the periphery of your vision until you notice and go after them or make the choice to turn a different direction. Once I got the puppy bug in my mind I couldn't stop thinking about them.

As you know, I own Dogaholics, and we had just pulled a large quantity of dog food to donate. I said to Jimmy, "You know, I have to take all this dog food to the dog shelter. Would you help me? And anyway, we could go and play with all these new puppies they just rescued." I had no intention of sharing with him my hope we would *get* a puppy.

He agreed, and we went and we met the puppies. Have you ever met a litter of puppies with complete objectivity?

Of course you haven't. That's impossible.

There was only one black one in the whole litter and his name was already Guinness. The lightest one—almost white—was Clover. We completely fell in love with them both.

They were my shiny object puppies, and I had already decided I needed them to come home with me. Jimmy took a little more convincing, but they glinted in his eye for a few hours and he succumbed to them, as well.

We went back to the shelter, got the puppies, signed all the paperwork, and headed home. We were still in the newness of attaining the shiny object, and it's lots of fun. Fortunately, owning a dog store, I was able to get a lot of our supplies right away (since we impulse-adopted), which made it an extra fun day (I mean, *shiny puppy accessories*, what's not to love?).

The next day we woke up to a strange sound in the kitchen. We walked out of the room, having forgotten there were these adorable little puppies in there, just looking at us with their cute little eyes. Now granted, they had chewed up all the paper, ripped up all the stuff, gone to the bathroom everywhere, and were soaking wet. Thank goodness they were cute.

Not to say we weren't very excited to have them, but with these little balls of energy standing before us, we had a big moment of *what have we done?*

Have you ever heard someone say they had "commitment issues"? We *all* have commitment issues when it comes to shiny objects, and it is step one to the chaos in our lives. We're attracted to shiny objects one after another. When the next one comes along, it's easy to lose the commitment to what you're supposed to be focusing on. Shiny Object Syndrome distracts us until we decide to focus on the new thing and let the other go.

When it comes to dogs, it's so easy to fall in love. It's easy to imagine the sweet puppy behind the shelter cage door as your companion for life. Visions of dog parks and fetched slippers dance in your head, and it's so much fun with a bubbly, bouncy puppy in your arms.

Until you wake up the next morning with your baseboards chewed off, your kitchen covered in pee, and the vet bill for shiny new puppy preventative care is more than your car payment.

You may not give them away (though according to the ASPCA over a million dogs are relinquished by their owners each year), but all too often once the shine wears off, pet parents lose focus on training their dogs and keeping them in the way they deserve to be kept. One of the biggest causes of dog behavior issues is a lack of follow-through from shiny object puppy to adult dog. A lot of other distractions came up, we're all busy, we didn't have time to commit, we meant to, but it got away from us.

Sound familiar?

Where in your life do you have shiny object syndrome?

_____

_____

_____

_____

What shiny objects are sitting in your car, your closet, on a shelf, or somewhere out of sight right now?

_____

_____

_____

What was the last shiny object you fixated on, and why?

_____

_____

_____

_____

Was the cost, time, or energy worth it? Why or why not?

_____

_____

_____

_____

Poor Planning

As humans, we're often attracted to potential. We're excited by the idea of a better, easier, more fulfilling future because we have or do something. We tend to be sold on the idea without always planning for the actual implementation, and we make choices which get us in trouble. When we fail to plan for our choices, distractions and obstacles arise, and we lose focus and our commitment wavers.

I've often seen new customers come into my store very excited to get a dog, but clearly not ready for a dog. Their lifestyle isn't ready for a dog. Their living situation isn't ready for a dog. They're finances aren't ready for a dog. But, gosh, a dog is really going to make their life complete, so they get a dog. It happens a lot with younger 20-somethings who aren't yet established—maybe the job they have now leaves them home a lot, but when the next job comes along, they're working more and hadn't planned for the expense of the pet care services they now need. All too often, it means they give up the dog.

I also see it frequently (and understandably) when people decide to get a dog, but go into the shelter with no plan and fall in love with the wrong dog for their lifestyle or living situation. Maybe they choose a dog who needs a lot of exercise, but the person's a couch potato. Or maybe the person works too much for a dog who needs a lot of mental stimulation.

When I got Tyson, I was working for myself, so it was easy—I took him to work with me all the time. The trouble hit when an out of town wedding I had committed to attend came up. I had Tyson for maybe 2 weeks, and the day before the wedding it occurred to me—what am I going to do with Tyson?

I had made no arrangements whatsoever. I was young—22—but still old enough to know better. I wasn't used to having a pet at all, and my life was so *busy*. I realized I had made all the necessary plans for *me*—getting a hotel room, the wedding was far and driving home would be out of the question—but I had no one to come and watch my dog. I didn't even have a dog walker because I took my dog to work with me. I had not made arrangements for the care of this pet who was completely dependent on me.

It was a shock! Here I thought I was this really responsible person, I was a great new dog owner, but I had completely forgotten to account for the fact I had this living being in my life, and when I wasn't around, who would care for my dog?

The chaos from poor planning shows up when we make two specific choices in a row. First, we don't plan ahead and make the right decision. We're human, and as much as we may learn from our mistakes, we're *not always going to make the right decision*. Fortunately, it doesn't mean we're doomed to chaos.

Second, we compound the wrong decision by refusing to make a plan for the decision we made, even if or *because* it wasn't ideal to begin with. Yes, you can salvage some of these decisions and shiny objects. It is not too late to plan now, even if your decision was made and you're in the midst of the consequences. We'll get to that in the next sections.

One of the most wide-spread, culturally-endorsed mechanisms of poor planning is debt and consumption. People buy things, take trips, and consume on a level they have no ability to pay for with no plan beyond the minimum payment. They buy homes that are too large and can't keep up with the responsibilities. Even when they make sufficient money to pay the debt, everything they buy creates more responsibility in care, time, and commitment. Acquiring *things* and obligations without planning costs dearly in time – time that takes away from time you could be spending doing other things – the things you really want to do.

Over-committing in this way without planning leaves people responsibility-heavy and thus constantly reacting to things. Their time is spent putting out fires rather than sitting down, creating an actual plan, and making sure they're following it to achieve their goals. They feel very *busy*, and are often running from one thing to the next, putting things in order, taking care of obligations, making sure things get done and happen the way they're supposed to.

You should never confuse *busy* with accomplishment. Never. Oftentimes at the end of the day, *busy* people can't look back and say there are specific things they made happen. When every day is spent reacting to each new crisis, people think they don't have time to plan, because gosh they have so much to do. They often find when they DO plan, all of a sudden they have so much *time*. Where did it come from?

I'm a bit of a workaholic, but I'm lucky because I love what I do. For a long time it was very easy for me to go years without taking time off or taking vacations. I'm always happy to go, but I often fell into the trap of plan-avoidance. I would say, "Great, plan it! I'll show up."

When I would get there and have a chance to disconnect from all of my "fires," I'd say "This sounds like fun. Let's do this, let's do that!" and invariably my travelling companions would reply, "It'd have been nice for you to have told us when we were planning, but THIS is what we're doing because you didn't give us any feedback when we were making these decisions."

So again, I missed out, and until I got this under control in my life, I didn't even get the opportunity to be excited about the vacation because I was trying to get all the other minutia in place and all the fires put out before I left.

For my business, I missed promotional marketing, free press, free opportunities to get in front of a new audience because I didn't plan far enough in advance to submit by deadlines. So many of us relate to the work-life "hamster wheel" when you're dealing so much *in* your business you don't have time to work *on* your business.

When the consequences of my lack of planning show up, it makes me wonder *what else am I missing out on?*

What have *you* missed out on?

What in your life should you have planned better?

_____

_____

_____

_____

What opportunities in your life have you missed out on because you didn't plan?

_____

_____

_____

_____

What would you have done differently?

_____

_____

_____

_____

What would your life look like today if you had committed to that decision?

_____

_____

_____

_____

Lack of Consistency

How many times have you been gung-ho to start a new project? It's so exciting and new in the beginning, but then *life happens* and you skip a little, slack a little, until you find yourself back with your fireman uniform on, putting out fires rather than making good choices for yourself, your dog, and your time. No matter how good your goal, no matter how much you've planned, no matter how *right* it is, a lack of consistency will derail you every time.

If our lives were exactly the same every day, it would be easy, but it's not. Our schedules change, the weather changes, our friends and family interrupt, people get hurt, people get sick, we get sick, finances get tight. Consistency means you can adapt to changes and still keep your commitments.

I'm always amazed at people who go to a conference or destination event, were up late working to catch up while out of town, and still get up and run 5 miles by the time the rest of the attendees are clutching coffee and working on their jet lag. Many of the rest of us might tell ourselves, "I'm not going to work out when I'm out of town." (Sound like anyone you know?)

Consistency is really about committing *daily* and in every situation. Before you can become consistent, you have to understand why you want what you want, because that has to be the yardstick you use to measure each choice. Is this choice in line with my goals? If not, how can I make it line up? Our morning conference runners have to evaluate their goals—the goals for the work event, the goals for their fitness program, the goals for their day, and make a decision that serves them. You can't just say "Oh, well I didn't bring my shoes so I can't run" or "Oh, I'll just skip." Consistency is saying "I'm going to take a break for this event. When I get back, in order to make it up, I'm going to do X." And then *doing it.*

If you've tried training your dog, but haven't seen the kinds of results you've wanted, I'm going to go out on a limb here and guess 99% of your problem has been your lack of consistency. If your dog is barking, you have to acknowledge it every time and correct it every time, because if you let it slide *sometimes*, they're going to say, "Oh, she let it slide this time, I guess it's okay forever. Yay!"

I live in a city where most of us don't have backyards, so we're all out leash-walking our dogs. Walks are fun, right? The dog gets to smell all the different smells, you get some exercise, maybe there'll be a squirrel or an alley cat, it's great.

Tell me if this sounds familiar. When you grab the leash to take your dog for a walk, they go bananas. If you have more than one, the dogs are jumping on top of each other, wrestling, one's giving love bites, everything devolves into happy chaos. And initially, you kind of allowed it (it's okay to admit). You encouraged the behavior, "Yeah! Isn't this fun? Let's go for a WALK!" I did it with Guinness and Clover – these are 60lb dogs. It started silly with everybody running down the stairs, we're leashing up, they're wrestling, I fall down, you know the drill. But the fun doesn't last, does it?

Pretty soon it got really annoying, and I couldn't believe it was still happening. Isn't this puppy behavior? Sheesh, calm down already! You're 6 years old. So let's say, like me, you fixed it. You got the tools and you made the crazy pre-walk chaos cease. But then when they started to behave well, it was easy to lose focus and stop being consistent with the effort, and that's where the little slacking off started to happen. I know you've seen this.

When you leash a dog up, it's a reward to get to go on a walk. Ideally, you shouldn't even leash them up until they're behaving exactly the way you want them to behave. They need to be in a calm sit position, and then you reward them with putting on the leash. It can be a long process, and when you live in the city you're looking at going through it *consistently* four times a day.

When you forget because you're focused on something else, or you're in a huge hurry and let it slide, everything you had worked up to--every time you had done the training with them, it was almost as if you just threw it out the window. In their minds, you were breaking the rule, and it told them, "Ooh! I guess the rule doesn't matter anymore!"

Our dogs are so much smarter than we give them credit for. Consider who else can do this, too. Your kids pick up on it, your coworkers, and your spouse!

Consistency is *hard*. Jumping back in when you have not been consistent is even harder—for you *and* for your dog. Just think about going back to the gym after travelling – you haven't worked out in two weeks, and you know you have to get back into the routine again. Those first days can feel impossible. It's so much easier to let it slide further and further.

With our dogs especially, we can also be plagued with a lack of consistency when we don't communicate effectively with the other people in our lives who will be caring for our dogs. When they display bad behaviors while you're gone, do your pet-caregivers or other family members know how to handle it? Consistency is not just about what you do, it's about ensuring everyone in your dog's life knows how to be consistent with your dog.

Lack of consistency is insidious. We may have planned an impeccable system or way of doing things; we may have implemented it and communicated it clearly, but without consistent effort and maintenance to it entropy will take over. Disorder will ensue. We give in to our schedules, the weather, our friends; we give in to the desire to do something we want to do instead of putting in the work and being consistent with our commitments to ourselves.

What goals did you have for your dog when they joined your family?

_____

_____

_____

_____

How would your relationship with your dog be today if you had stuck with those goals?

_____

_____

What goals have you set for yourself that you started working toward, but did not complete?

_____

_____

_____

_____

Wastefulness

Wastefulness can happen easily, and often because we're not paying attention. As pet owners, we're the newest it-group for consumerism. Nobody knows it more than I do. I'm a pet-parent with a pet store! I see all the coolest stuff at the trade shows, and as a *dogaholic,* I love to try things. The chaos shows up because there are always going to be *problem-solving products,* but unless we actually use them consistently (...are you sensing a theme?), they'll never work.

I think we've all been guilty of buying an amazing product we're excited about, but we don't end up using it. How many times do we get something, use it about a week, have to wash it and there it sits for a month, or leave it at someone's house, or leave it in our car?

I hear from clients every day who experience the same thing with their pets. For example, we carry an amazing product called the Thundershirt. It's a tight wrap to calm dogs down and help with anxiety (and for our Chicago storms, it's a must-have for nervous dogs in the summertime). It's great, truly useful, but *you have to remember to put it on your dog.* We buy quick fixes for our problems, but don't follow through on the learning curve or process to really see results.

How many people buy fitness gadgets because everyone says how great they are? You become invested in the idea of the person you'll be with a FitBit, and you buy one. *Maybe I'll lose weight with a FitBit. Maybe I'll get healthier.* How many of you have a FitBit in a drawer you stopped wearing or never could figure out how to hook up to your phone? How many people do you know who were surprised they need to actually *use* it consistently for their fitness gadget to work?

So many of us have gym memberships and don't go to the gym, automated payments to services we stopped using, money and energy going out, out, out, without a benefit coming back to us. We consume, throw away, have no value for many things, because we've become disconnected from the money we earn and spend. Between direct deposit, paying online, credit cards, gift cards, etc, it makes it easy for money to come and go without us realizing it. We never see it unless we check our bank account. And how often do most of us do *that?*

I see dogs come into the store with owners who aren't paying attention. The dog starts chewing on something the owner didn't plan to buy, and it's "Oh, well, I guess we have to buy it now." It *can be* a good scenario—it's fun to shop in the store with your dog and make him happy, but the wastefulness from simply not paying attention can get quickly out of hand.

First, the dog chews one and *okay I'll buy one*. Then, they're not paying attention and the dog goes after another. We've seen dogs steal up to four of our pork hearts! It's usually big Labradors the owners can't control and they say *no-no*, and tighten up the leash, but never get the dog to sit. While they're trying to pay for the one, the dog keeps going back because *the owner just doesn't have control*.

When was the last time you balanced your checking account? Why?

_____

_____

_____

Do you have any subscriptions, automatic payments, or memberships you pay for but don't regularly use?

_____

_____

_____

Is there any part of your consumption habits you feel like you have no control over?

_____

_____

_____

How many products have you purchased for yourself or for your dog you don't regularly use? What made you buy them? What made you stop using them?

_____

_____

_____

These Four Dogs Travel in a Pack

When you reflect on the chaos in your life and have to ask yourself "How did this happen," it's because all these things are happening simultaneously. They blindside you—you don't even know they're happening because they're *everywhere* and *everybody does it*. Our dogs are not immune, and also not equipped to make the kinds of choices we can to counteract it.

My dog Clover is obsessed with tennis balls. She has shiny tennis ball syndrome. She can't listen, can't think, can't focus on anything else. If there is a tennis ball around, she loses her mind. What about your dog? Is it squirrels? Other dogs?

We have to be their higher order thinking skills for them. They can't plan, they have no bank account, they have no ability to make these kinds of decisions like we do. *They can't make a daily choice*. We have to make that choice for them. If we are not able to make it in our own lives—if we have a shiny tennis ball syndrome except with fitness gadgets or apps, or whatever our thing is—then there's no way our dog is going to be able to deal or behave the way we'd like them to. We brought them into our lives, we need to recommit to them because they can't fend for themselves. We made the decision to be responsible for them.

We have all these distractions and our lack of commitment affects our lives so much; imagine how much it affects theirs.

I know, because I was suffering under these four chaotic influences for a long time. When I started the business, I worked, worked, worked, and eventually I had to make some tough decisions about how I was spending my time. I started planning a lot more and I made the choice to spend a lot of time with my dogs. I made choices that served my goals instead of my passing fancies. I chose to be consistent with myself and my dogs, and a good steward of our resources.

In 2014, I lived my best life. I learned how to be so aware of how we fall into these traps and how harmful it is to your well-being and what you really want. All of these things are pulling at you: shiny object syndrome, lack of planning, lack of consistency, and wastefulness. They drain your energy and leave you living a life you don't really want. You wake up one day and find yourself living a life based on all the decisions and obligations and *things* you brought into your life – the chaos. You've brought it in, and too often you do it *accidentally*.

We make purchases based on emotional decisions and desires, causing financial burdens. We get a dog without thinking about where our life is headed and if the dog will fit into our lifestyle. They're still decisions *even if you didn't make them* – even if you just let them be made.

I really didn't have time to have two puppies. It was a purely emotional decision. They were so cute, so I let my emotional response to those shiny puppies override what I knew to be the right decision. I saw "signs" in their names, I *bonded* with them. I didn't think about the future or the responsibilities of two puppies who would grow into two dogs with two vet bills and two food bills. I ignored the fact that every puppy is cute. I ignored the fact I that could name *any* puppy an Irish name. I chose to forget that if you put me in a room with 112 dogs, I would probably be able to bond with all of them. None of it mattered. I wanted THOSE puppies. Shiny, shiny puppies.

It was fun! We took them outside, we took them on walks, we began to work on training. I took them to my store; I introduced them to my customers. Everyone got to meet them. Everyone loved them.

Training, however, was not going as smoothly as we'd hoped. At only two weeks in, it was really putting a strain on our marriage, because I was running a business and we were both working a lot, and we didn't have a ton of time to be devoted to training the puppies. And puppies—even when they come in singles—take a lot of time and effort. Because we had two, it was overwhelming.

As I said before, the chaos comes in when you make two specific choices in a row: the choice to not plan ahead and the refusal to make a plan for the decision you made, even if or *because* it wasn't ideal to begin with.

Jimmy finally reached his breaking point and came to me very upset and said "I think you need to give one of these puppies back. This just isn't going to work." I was devastated. I had already bonded with them; I didn't want to give them up. I had already introduced them to my customers—here I own a dog business, sit on the board of the rescue, and hold values in direct conflict with this, and I'm supposed to just say now, "It was too tough for me so I gave a dog back."

I had to say *I don't care if it's hard. I have to find a way to make it work.*

These four traps go so well together because they're all intertwined. We like to look for quick and easy fixes for our problems, the shiny objects we believe will make our lives better. We act on impulse and forget to (or refuse to) plan. We flake out on our commitments because new distractions come up, and we waste our resources starting back at the beginning chasing more shiny objects. If we don't become aware of these traps, we'll never escape them – and since we're living in a culture that rewards these behaviors, it's a *commitment* to choose a different path.

We frequently get customers in the store who come in and say things like, "I want a leash that will stop my dog from pulling" and we have to say, "Well, there's no leash that will stop your dog from pulling. There are some harnesses and gentle leaders that will help and aid in it, but it really comes down to the person, not the dog."

You can imagine the looks we get. We continue, "It comes down to the person committing to working on the heel command, getting treats, being consistent on every walk, getting the dog to focus on you, to have more attention on you than on any distractions he's pulling towards on the street. You need to figure out *why* your dog is pulling and get in control."

The usual response? "Oh, that's not going to work for me. I'm going to find a leash that's going to stop my dog from pulling."

And we wish them good luck.

Pet Parent Bonding Activity

Look around your home and find any "shiny objects" you bought for your dog, and make a point to use them this week. Decide which ones you want to keep and which you could give away.

It's a great opportunity to play and connect with your dog, but will also help bring consciousness to any other items that might have been a wasteful decision.

Don't get sidetracked with cleaning up the clutter! Remember this *to-do* is for *your pup's stuff*. Schedule closet cleaning for a later time.

CHAPTER THREE

How Did I Find Myself Here? It's All in Your Head

"How many legs does a dog have if you call the tail a leg? Four. Calling a tail a leg doesn't make it a leg." –Abraham Lincoln

It's well-documented that dog lovers are the best kind of people—friendly, forgiving, fun, and just downright superior. It's great, of course, but this sort of friendly mental space also has some major drawbacks.

Look at your dog. When you mess up, what does your dog think about it? Do you get a strongly-worded letter detailing how there is no actual meat in the food you bought him, and how "because it was on sale" is not a valid reason to choose it? Does she present you with an Excel spreadsheet detailing the decline in average minutes per walk over the last three months? Does he pick up the slack and sign himself up for a training class since you haven't had time to call during business hours?

Nope.

If your dog could speak, she'd say, "It's okay! Love you anyway! Scratch my ear! What's in your pocket? Are you going to finish your hot dog?"

Dog people tend to be forgiving, even to a fault. That's why we love our dogs who love us unconditionally. I mean, we *get* them. We *get* unconditional. We give the benefit of the doubt, and we assume the best in people until they prove us wrong.

Unfortunately because of this, we are some of the worst offenders when it comes to letting chaos into our lives from the inside out. We give ourselves too much leniency, we give our dogs too much leniency, and we compound those four commitment traps from the last chapter with mental attitudes doing us (and our dogs) no favors.

When these hit close to home, just remember: kindness is best expressed with the truth. Even to ourselves. Are you ready for some tough love?

You'll be fine. Here, have the rest of my hot dog. I was saving it for you.

Head in the Sand

Have you ever seen a puppy with an older dog? The puppy bobs and weaves and jumps and yips and nips and rolls, and the older dog shoots you a long-suffering look as if to say, "Are you *kidding* me?" He turns away; he makes a dog-circle and buries his nose; he heads for his crate; he does anything he can to ignore this furry nuisance who is, for some unknown reason, bouncing on his head.

How well do you think it works?

As any old dog who has suffered through the puppy phase can tell you, the only thing to do about their "puppy problem" is to offer a swift correction, repeated as necessary until the problem comes under control. How many times have we buried our noses (or our whole heads) when faced with a problem rather than taking the swift correction route?

We think we're waiting until we're ready. We figure the problem or chaos will go away if we ignore it. We think someone else will deal with it—everything from continuing to put more trash in an already overfull trash can to our out of control finances.

Even the biggest dog-lovers regularly fall into this trap. It's exciting and fun to get a puppy; they're amazing little creatures full of love, joy, and wonder at the world. It's easy to ignore their exuberance and think, "Oh, it's just a puppy thing; it's going to stop." And yes, they may slow down a bit, but the reason why older dogs have it down is because (for the most part) their people taught them.

With Clover and Guinness, they obviously learned how to go to the bathroom outside and they learned to sit and they are good dogs, but when they were puppies, they were often kept in the kitchen when they were on their own in the early stages. My adorable puppies ripped up paper towels and toilet paper rolls. They completely chewed off the baseboards around the entire kitchen, pulled the doorframes off, chewed up the tile, and scratched up things. Guinness was so smart he learned how to pop the gates open and walk through the rooms because he saw us do it so many times.

I can't tell you how many wonderful, loving pet-parent customers have come into my store with adult dogs who continue this behavior far past the puppy phase, thinking it's eventually going to end. I crate trained Guinness and Clover early because of this, but not in time to save my kitchen! So many new dog owners are resistant to crate training because they feel like it's punishment for what is, ostensibly, normal puppy behavior. It's not, of course, it's giving them a safe place all their own — they really need it. But when we figure the behaviors will stop, we aren't proactive in finding a solution.

Often in the beginning, a new puppy gets treated like a human family member: they sleep on the couch or in bed with you, and isn't it so cute how they gobble up the table scraps and fight with the tissue box? But then all of a sudden they weigh 50, 70, 100lbs, and it's not so cute when they hog your bed and can rest their head on the dining room table while standing comfortably next to you during dinner.

Collection agencies exist because of head-in-the-sand actions. People make a choice they shouldn't have, become afraid to face it, and hope it'll go away. You know it's your fault for having made these decisions (hopefully you know it's your fault – if not, I'm telling you it is), but you either feel entitled and believe someone else is going to handle it or you think it's not as big of a deal as it is. You deny it affects other people or think will just go away, but it won't.

When we just acknowledge the problems, acknowledge the situation we're in and take action, then just like puppy training, we can solve the problem.

Let's say you owed money. If you ignore it, they're going to take whatever measures they need to take because they can't get in touch with you. Those measures are often drastic and come with brand new consequences and difficulties for you (kind of like crate training a 100lb dog for the first time - try it). If you just reach out and make a plan you show good faith, and they know you're working with them. They know you are trying to get out of your situation and you can work together to get through it.

If you ignore it, the problem you had on day 1 is not the same problem you will have on day 60. It will be bigger, hairier, and much harder to control.

Your ability to face your problems or the results of choices you made is a reflection of your integrity. Whether you like it or not, choosing to put your head in the sand tells everyone (especially anyone also affected by your choices) you don't keep your word, and *they aren't valuable to you*. Whether this is your spouse or family, your children, or your dog, this mental block lets you off the hook...but only temporarily...and magnifies the problems you're trying to avoid. It's easier to teach a 20lb puppy to heel than it is to do the same with a 100lb adult dog. You still have to do it either way, so make your choice.

What problems with your dog have you ignored, thinking they'll go away on their own?

_____

_____

_____

_____

How have those problems changed and intensified over time?

_____

_____

_____

_____

What would your life with your dog look like today if you had addressed those problems early on?

_____

_____

_____

_____

Where in your life have you ignored a problem (or where are you ignoring one even today)?

_____

_____

_____

_____

What is keeping you from addressing the problem and finding a solution?

_____

_____

_____

_____

Making Excuses

You may think you hold the title, but I was the queen of
busy. My biggest excuse for anything I didn't get done was I was
just so, so busy. I had a business with lots of employees, a
family, two dogs, volunteer work, occasionally I had to sleep
and eat, and even those were often done on the run. It wasn't
an *excuse*, it was my life! Right? I just have so much on my plate
(because I said YES instead of NO), there just wasn't enough
time in the day, but that didn't mean I couldn't try! You with
me?

It was an excuse. And if the *queen* of busy can own it,
you can, too.

I had a realization after missing yet another deadline
where I had to say, "I'm so sorry, I was just so busy! Where did
the time go?" I was living behind the excuse of *I'm sorry, I'm so
busy*. My entire existence came down to rushing around and
apologizing for it, because as busy as I was, things weren't
getting done. If these commitments I was making had really
mattered to me, I would have blocked out the time and gotten
them done.

And the worst part? I was basically showing the people,
pets, and plans I committed to that *they didn't matter*.

With Guinness and Clover, though I crate trained,
taught them where to go potty, and made sure they could sit,
my *busy* derailed the rest of the training they should have had
until much, much later. We signed up for a training class, but

both Jimmy and I needed to commit and make time for it—two dogs, two people to manage and work with each dog.

We went to the first class, were so excited about the things we would learn, and the puppies got mange. Mange! As shelter puppies who had spent a lot of their early weeks in between who knows where and their shelter homes, they picked up some yucky stuff, and there we were with two mangy mutts (cute ones, but mangy). They couldn't be around other dogs, so we had to halt the training until it cleared up, which turned into years (would anyone believe we were just waiting a few years extra to make sure they *really* weren't contagious?).

The *busy* reared its ugly head for both of us. Jimmy couldn't commit to coming to the training and I was so *busy* with all of my other commitments, I couldn't follow through with the commitments to my dogs. We got completely off course, and it all fell apart.

Your excuse may not be busy, though it is one of the biggest (my queendom is large and heavily populated). How about "I work too much – I don't have a great relationship with my kids, because I work so much. I do it for them! They've got such a great life and have everything I never had. My spouse picks up the slack, and they know I love them. I just don't really know them all that well. They're great kids, though."

Yours may be "I can't go do this activity; I can't go to the show; I can't take a vacation, because gosh, I just don't have the money." Sometimes it's gone before you get it—spent on the obligations you've made without considering the consequences to your life. Sometimes your broke mindset tells you since you have so little money, might as well indulge in something small like a fancy coffee. You continue believing you *can't afford* to take a vacation or invest in yourself, not thinking through the reality: if you stopped spending $5-7 dollars a day on those little indulgences, you'd have $150 each month to put toward something that truly fulfils you.

We're equal opportunity excusers, so we let our dogs off the hook for some surprisingly common reasons. And really, if we're being honest, letting our dogs off the hook is really letting *us* off the hook – for their training, their proper care, or their sociability. Truth is kindness, remember. I never said this would be easy.

My dog's just a puppy! He'll grow out of it. My dog is too old, she can't learn, she's done this her whole life. She's used to the food, I don't want to change it on her now. My dog's lazy, he won't want to walk. My dog is fine! That's just how dogs are. Or even, the ever-shocking: My dog's a rescue. He can't learn. He lived in a shelter for too long. He's always going to bark at people, and he's never going to like men because he's a rescue...which, by the way, is a big lie you're telling yourself.

Let me get this out of the way first: yes, there is room for extreme issues or deep behavioral problems caused by years of abuse. Absolutely, there are going to be those situations. However, it doesn't mean those situations can't be helped, and those situations are fewer and farther between than we'd like to think when we make these excuses for our dogs.

Instead of working on the root of what's going on and getting consistent in the training to change the behavior, we make these excuses (and so many more I can't list here or it'd just be 100 pages of excuse note).

What we find at Dogaholics is if the issue takes more than a few minutes or a quick and easy product to solve, too many people are not interested in the solution. They'd rather live with the problem and tell themselves the excuses to try and make it okay. I'm not immune, and there is a solution (or I wouldn't be writing this book). What we need is a strong enough motivator to change, and strangely enough, so do our dogs.

Let me tell you about Clover. She doesn't like biscuit treats—you can drive through the bank line with her, and she couldn't care less about their big jar in the window. I found with normal training, chicken jerky was her *thing*, and she'd happily obey for more of it. Usually.

Enter the Chicago squirrel population.

They're furry, they're cute, and they turn Clover into a raving dog maniac. The chicken jerky was just not cutting it. We'd be out on a walk, a squirrel would move into her field of vision, and she would *take me down* in relentless pursuit of those little rodents. I tried; I waved the chicken jerky like a white flag of squirrel truce, but it wasn't a big enough motivator to get her behavior to change.

I had a choice. I could say, "Oh, she's just obsessed with squirrels, and there's nothing I can do but hang on. It's just who she is." Or I could find another treat more enticing than the squirrel. Turns out, for Clover, it's dried lamb lung, and she can't resist it. And all the squirrels in Wrigleyville sent me little thank you notes.

Too often, we give into an excuse like, "Oh, he's not food motivated, so we can't work on training because it just doesn't work for me" instead of taking the time to find out what really motivates their dog. Some dogs are motivated by love and affection—Guinness likes treats, but he'd also be happy if I just gave him a good scratch and made eye contact or praised him verbally if he did something great.

Whether the excuse is for you or your dog, it comes down to choice and personal effort. Either you make the choice to make it a priority or you refuse to figure it out, make an excuse, and say, "It just doesn't matter to me." Making excuses boils down to you not willing to do the work. (And before you say you don't know *how* to do the work, I've got you covered. Keep reading.)

Why can't your dog behave in the way you want him/her to?

_____

_____

_____

How much time and effort have you devoted to finding and implementing a solution?

_____

_____

_____

_____

Be honest – no one will read this but you – are you making excuses for your dog's behavior? Why?

_____

_____

_____

_____

What excuses have you fallen back on in your non-dog life? Are they similar?

_____

_____

_____

_____

Enabling

I'm not sure if you're aware of this, and I know for some of you it will come as a great shock, but your dogs are not humans.

I know, I know! It's revolutionary and feels strange to admit (after all, I know some of you have the "Dogs are People, Too" t-shirt and wear it proudly), but it is good for you and good for your dogs to acknowledge it and let it inform your choices.

We humanize our dogs daily. They're on our couches, they get to sleep in our beds. I'm not naming names (you know who you are), but some of you let your dogs sip out of your lattes and take bites of your ice cream.

Listen, I don't mean to call you out or call any of these things specifically bad behaviors (except the lattes, dogs and coffee don't really go together), but the problem and chaos come in when we don't make these as choices – or the choices we make for our dogs are based on the assumption they're humans like us. Just slightly less evolved. And furrier. When we don't acknowledge our dogs are dogs, we enable behaviors that are harmful to them and to us. We can treat them like family—we *should* treat them like family—but they are canine members, not human, and they have different needs.

We frequently hear our customers ask about problems they're having with their dogs due to lack of structure and lack of rules. When the pups rule the roost, suddenly it's not such a hospitable home for the people. If the dog knows his boundaries, he keeps to them. If he has no boundaries, he becomes the boss. (And frankly, unless he's Lassie and paying the mortgage, that's a problem.)

We come by this innocently enough. We seek love and affection from our dogs. They help us manage our own insecurities, they lift us up, they make us feel special in a way other humans (with their own insecurities and foibles) have a harder time expressing. When our desire for love and affection make us break the household rules, our dogs will soon disregard the rules completely. We see it with our human children when we want to be the "cool" mom or dad, so we buy too much or allow too much. We give them the tools of their own destruction when we enable: entitlement, wastefulness, lack of appreciation, lack of gratitude, lack of humility. Now apply this to your dog, who you've humanized into a four-legged child, and you can see how your happy house can get out of control.

When we enable our dogs, it comes in several forms. Recently there has been a huge number of incredibly obese pets taking the national attention through social media and the viral spread of news. These pets almost all had owners who showed love to their pets through food. They ate whenever they wanted, they were fed indulgent people-food, and soon they were loved almost to death.

We've all been to homes where the owner spent more time apologizing for the dog's behavior than entertaining his or her guests. The big dogs whose noses constantly find their way where no noses should go; the dogs who jump excitedly on unsuspecting people who walk in the door; the dogs who bark their welcome to every falling leaf outside the window—and they wonder why no one comes to visit a second time. Let's meet somewhere for coffee instead. Right?

These same owners are often unwilling (calling themselves unable) to crate train because they think it's cruel. "My dog is very sensitive. She didn't take well to the crate." Or "My dog was in a shelter; I don't want him to have any more time in a cage."

Do you have established house rules? Why or why not? If you do, do you always follow them?

_____

_____

_____

_____

Are you guilty of allowing your dog to act in ways that conflict
with your goals for their behavior? How? Explain it to yourself.

_____

_____

_____

_____

Oblivious to the Problems

You may have heard of the four stages of competence developed in the 1970's by Gordon Training International, and now an integral part of our cultural understanding of learning a new skill. They are:

- Unconscious Incompetence
- Conscious Incompetence
- Conscious Competence
- Unconscious Competence

In recent years, many authors and thinkers have tacked on a fifth stage—one I'll be talking about later in the book. Dog owners (or the rest of us in our day-to-day lives) often get stuck lower on the scale and find it nearly impossible to move forward. The problems we face, both dog-related and not, can never be addressed if we don't even recognize there is a problem.

Unconsciously incompetent is the oblivious state. You don't know it's rude for your dog to jump up on people. (Maybe I'm surprising you by talking about these things as problems. Maybe someone gifted you this book, and you're still not sure why...) You don't know what you don't know or what you *should know*, so you can't even figure out how to access the right information. Maybe you grew up where your dogs jumped up on everybody. When you got a dog, you didn't realize the dog's jumping isn't okay. You've got chaos stemming from it, but don't recognize there's a problem. Chaos is where you live and what you know. If you're here, your first goal is to bring consciousness to what it is you want to improve and why.

Maybe you do know there's a problem, but you don't know how to fix it (or worse, don't care). If so, you're **consciously incompetent**. You may make excuses for your dog (or for you), you may be too busy or your dog untrainable. You may know training works, but not for *your* dog. You recognize that you and your dog are not living the way you should, and you have a vision of what it would look like if you fixed these issues. You might not know how to fix it yet, or you might think you're not able to fix it, but at least you're bringing awareness to it and can seek out solutions (that's why you're here, right?).

Too many dog owners stay incompetent by choice or because they're oblivious to their own lack of knowledge. In the next section, I'll talk about the next three stages, and how you can live there instead of staying stuck in incompetence.

Do you fall into one of the first two stages of competence with your dog? Which one? Why?

_____

_____

_____

If you don't recognize yourself in one of the first two stages, can you remember a time when you were? What was the catalyst which helped you move beyond?

_____

_____

_____

Paralyzed by Fear

Doesn't it just break your heart when people are irrationally afraid of dogs? Maybe they experienced a trauma as a child, maybe they get the heebie-jeebies from Scooby Doo, and maybe they've been jumped on and sniffed and barked at by too many big, out of control dogs. It's hard for us, those who know what our relationships with our dogs give us, to see them missing out on it because of fear.

If we look a little closer, we can empathize. Why? Because we are limited by our own fear more often than we'd care to admit.

How many times have you limited your own activity or forward motion because you worry and overthink? How often has anxiety come up because you can't get out of your own head, even just to figure out where the anxiety is *really* coming from? How often has the anxiety cycle made you shut down and not have the clarity to push through to your end goal?

Whether you'd love to have a dog you can take to the dog park or a life and career you'd love to wake up to every morning, the fear is the same. Ask yourself: am I really afraid of failure (What if it doesn't work? What if I do all this work and my dog still freaks out and attacks another dog at the dog park?) or afraid of success (What will have to change in my life if I achieve this? What will I no longer be able to use as an excuse if this works? What else will I have to admit and commit to?).

Self-doubt and self-criticism are a form of self-abuse. When we let fear control us, however our fear manifests, we are sabotaging our life. By refusing to make the commitment to the things we want, we are living like the person afraid of dogs — never knowing what joy and fulfilment we could have in our lives if we would just step outside of our comfort zone.

What are you afraid of when it comes to your dog's behavior? What is the worst that could happen?

_____

_____

_____

What is most likely to happen?

_____

_____

_____

_____

What are you afraid of in your non-dog life situation? What is
the worst that could happen?

_____

_____

_____

_____

What is most likely to happen?

_____

_____

_____

_____

If you didn't experience the fear, how would your life and your
dog's life be different right now?

_____

_____

_____

_____

Pet Parent Bonding Activity

Take out a piece of paper or turn on whatever gadget you use and make a list. This list will be your "House Rules" for your dog. Decide what is allowed and what is not allowed. Write out the commands everyone will use to correct bad behavior and reward good ones. Post and share them with all other members in your household and any pet sitters.

Now, start living by this "House Rules" list. If everyone is on the same page, there can be no more excuses about why the dog is on the couch again if he's not supposed to be there.

Part Two:

Throw Yourself A Bone

It's Not the Size of the Dog in the Fight, It's the Size of the Fight in the Dog

"Blame is just a lazy person's way of making sense of chaos. "
-Douglas Coupland

I'd like to clear up a common misconception that seems to plague us like a little flea-biting on the coat. Just when you think you're comfortable, it makes itself known. No matter how hard you scratch, you can't seem to get rid of it. Well, consider this your flea dip.

You're not lazy. You may have acted lazy in the past, but you are not actually lazy at all. Lazy is an excuse, and it's hardly ever a true one. You're a thoughtful, caring pet parent, and you're reading this book to help change the situation you and your dog are in. If you were lazy, you wouldn't be here.

We get dissatisfied with our lives, but won't do anything to change it. We stay in jobs we hate because it's easier than making a change. It's scary to move outside our comfort zone, even when our comfort zone isn't so comfortable.

I've had to make the choice to ignore fear, because I know I'm the only person who can change my situation. I'm the only person in my life who *cares* about *my life*. Nobody is going to look out for me the way I will. I need to love myself more than anyone in the world loves me, because I'm the only one who can make my life what I want it to be. My dog can't make these choices; I have to make them for him.

In this section, I'm going to show you how to connect with your vision, find your motivation, and ditch the lazy excuse for the rest of your life. You are the only one who has the power to make these changes – for you and for your dog. You're both worth it. Let's go.

CHAPTER FOUR

If You're Looking For the Problem, Find a Mirror

"It is a truism to say that the dog is largely what his master makes of him: he can be savage and dangerous, untrustworthy, cringing and fearful; or he can be faithful and loyal, courageous and the best of companions and allies."
–Sir Ranulph Fiennes

We've spent a lot of time going through the ways we get distracted, the ways we lose our focus and motivation, and the ways we bail on our commitments. I know you've seen yourself in some (many? all?) of them, but I also know our first instinct is never to own our mistakes and work to correct them. Our first instinct is to retreat into those same chaos-contributors and hunker down to weather the storm.

As clear as if you were standing in front of me, I can hear some of you right now, "Well, okay. But my dog is different. He's one of those exceptions you talked about before. And I really am busy, but it's *real* busy and not just an excuse."

Before you can find motivation, before you can set a goal and learn how to achieve it, before you can be the best pet parent you can be, you have to understand you have a problem and acknowledge you have the power to fix it. Ultimately, it all comes down to you. Each problem comes from choices you make and influences you allow in. Knowing you are the architect of your own chaos *is power*, because it means you can also be the architect of your own success.

Busy is a choice. Lazy is a choice. Excuses are a choice.

Your dog can't make these choices, so it's imperative for you to make them for him. It's critical to become aware of the traps along the way (especially the ones you've fallen into before), and make different choices now because *it's not too late*.

The title of this book tells you not to give up on your dogs, because by the time you get here, you may already be on that path. The end game of believing you are not in control of the chaos you've brought into your life is the relinquishment. I see it in my work at the rescue as well as with a very small percentage of my store customers.

Here's how it usually goes. You made a decision to bring a dog into your life. You got the dog, you brought it into your house, and you made it a part of your family. You didn't train it—you were going to get around to it, but then it was "too late." A few years in, you bring a child into your family, you move, you get another dog, or you make a career change. You're around less, your attention is elsewhere, you don't transition the dog appropriately because it didn't occur to you that the living, breathing animal in your house may need to be guided into the new way of doing things.

New behavior issues crop up: anxiety, more protectiveness, accidents, separation anxiety, barking. Maybe they're sensing stress with you or other family members, and without a transition they're left to deal with it themselves.

Sometimes there are reactions where the dog will nip or growl at the new child or at you, maybe you see the behavior changes and you're just afraid something might happen, so you give up the dog because it no longer fits into your lifestyle.

Now, you may never get to that point, and you may look with shock and horror on the mere suggestion you would, but for over a million dogs a year, this is their reality.

Why? Because their humans thought they didn't have the power to change it. They thought they weren't in control. They thought it was too late to fix the issues, and they *gave up*. The shiny object lost its shine, and the solution was to find a new one. Even if you're not at such a dire point, it can be hard to acknowledge you can change your trajectory. Admitting you can is admitting you got yourself into it in the first place.

If what you're doing doesn't scare you a little, you're not reaching high enough.

Using the exercises in the last chapter, you've identified what's tripping you up—be it with your dog's behavior or your own life. Let's revisit the five stages of competence, and I'll show you how you've got the power to make this journey. Each step gains more control, more awareness, and more ability while leaving the excuses behind.

The Stages of Competence

To jog your memory, the four stages of competence are:

- Unconscious Incompetence
- Conscious Incompetence
- Conscious Competence
- Unconscious Competence

You remember the first two stages from the last chapter—the stages where you're living with the chaos and not sure how to get out of it. If you're living in unconscious incompetence, you're not even aware you have a problem, let alone how to fix it. Conscious incompetence has you stuck in your problem without the means or the desire to fix it. Neither are ideal, but the good news (if you're in one or the other) is there's a clear path *up*. You can't fix anything if you don't know it needs to be fixed. Once you are aware of the problem, even though you don't yet know how to fix it, you can find the solution. Both are stepping stones—just don't stay in the middle of the river too long.

Conscious competence begins when we know how to do something, but it takes effort and concentration every single time we do it. It is the process of unlearning the bad behavior (ours and our dog's). It's thinking through every step of our walk: they must be calm before we leash up, I must have them sit at each crosswalk, I bring out the treats when we go to the park because of the squirrels, I remind myself every few minutes to make sure he's staying in heel. You're aware of the problem, you know how to fix it, and you're consciously making the necessary changes. You're implementing the plan, and while you have to make a constant mental effort to stay on track, you (and your dog) are reaping the rewards.

Unconscious competence begins when you've mastered the new skill and can do it without even thinking. Your dog's usual reaction to you picking up the leash is to be calm. If he's having an off day, you automatically wait until he's ready without having to make an effort. Your hand goes to the treats in the park as if on cue. You know he's in heel, and he knows by your bearing to stay there. It doesn't matter when or where you walk, and it doesn't matter who is with you—human or canine—you have it down to the point of being unconscious. It's as natural to you as breathing.

Here's where the stages have expanded as more people have brought more focus on intention, and is ideal for both your journey with your dog and your journey in your life. For our purposes, we'll call it **Conscious Competence of Unconscious Competence.** This newer, fifth stage begins when you're setting a daily intention to live your best life, to reach your goals, to work toward something you know will fulfil you. It transcends the "automatic," and becomes a daily choice. You may have mastered the walk in the last stage, but here you reflect on it and you choose it consciously. You may be a walk expert who could do all the steps perfectly while asleep, but you choose to be awake and aware. You commit daily to your dog, and you reap the benefits of the relationship, your dog's health, and your dog's commitment to you. Your days and daily activities – even ones as mundane as quick walks for doggy bathroom breaks – no longer fly by in a blur. You don't look at your day and wonder what you did.

In this fifth stage, you can often teach others the skills you've mastered, as your intention and awareness of the process gives you clarity. Having seen and overcome the barriers, you can effectively navigate others past them.

This fifth stage is where you'll live your best life.

I'm going to explain this in relation to dog food. It's a little easier to digest than pet relinquishment, and I want you to see how these stages inform every decision you make for your dogs. Each moment with them is an opportunity for you to make choices, and the more you practice it with your dog, the more you find other areas of your life can't help but move up a stage. Try it!

Your dog is not choosing what to put in their food bowl. Nutrition and the quality of food you can give a dog is critical for their physical and mental health and well-being. You're the one going to the grocery store or pet store to pick out their food, and the choices you make affect you, as well. Studies have shown that having a dog decreases our stress, we have healthier hearts, we're more active, and we get big health benefits. Putting care and commitment into their system feeds us as well.

Unconsciously incompetent people have never read the ingredients on a bag of dog food. They assume if it's sold at their supermarket and has DOG on the package, it's adequate for their dog's needs. The dog eats it, so everything's fine. They'll switch occasionally to follow a coupon. They have no idea the food they're choosing is the human equivalent of a fast food experiment where every day is like eating from the drive through.

Consciously incompetent people have learned there are vast differences in dog food available. They may have learned what ingredients to look out for, but after looking at all the food at the supermarket, can't find one that fits the bill and don't know where else to go. Maybe they've decided they don't care enough to make a change, and continue buying what's on sale and readily accessible while they're doing their own grocery shopping.

Consciously competent people have discovered the local pet supply shop in their neighborhood and have chosen a biologically appropriate food which is efficient for their dog's systems. They've chosen a food with the nutrients to extend their dog's life and prevent health problems. It's more expensive than the grocery store brand, so they have to remember to budget and account for the cost each month. They've set a reminder on their phone to alert them every few weeks to pick some up so they don't forget and have to resort to the grocery store brand again.

Unconsciously competent people make an automatic Thursday trip to the store to grab the food. When they're going to be out of town, they stock up, and no matter what comes up during their day, they don't miss picking up the dog's food. It's a regular part of the household budget, and the cost is factored in with their regular monthly expenses without much thought.

People who are **consciously competent of their unconscious competence** make the same trip to the store, but they know the owner now and make a point to say hello and swap dog stories. They know the health benefits of the ingredients and choose between excellent foods based on their merits rather than choosing a good food over a poor one. They consider the act of feeding their dog a part of their daily commitment to his care, and they do it with intention and love. They freely share their knowledge in a kind and helpful way, not with judgment or criticism, as they remember the days when they'd add dog food to their shopping cart full of milk, bread, and eggs. They find the intentional way they feed their dog carries over into other choices they make for him – what products they use, what boarding facility they go to, what kind of veterinary care he receives – and in their own lives – what kind of career they want, how they interact with their family, how they spend their free time. Their life is really good, and they're happy more often than not.

It's easy to get bogged down in what brought you to this place. We are culturally conditioned by surviving decades of advertising and screen saturation to be easily distracted and malleable. It's in "their" best interest for you to consume more, excuse more, enable more, and stay stuck.

The fact is, you're emotionally creating your own barriers. Once you get out of your own way and see what's truly possible, you can live a guilt free life with integrity, joy, love and full experiences.

The fact that the problem is you is not an indictment of your choices—we've *all* made some doozies in our lives. The fact that the problem comes down to you is a *blessing* because it means *you have the power* to choose better now that you know better. And those choices add up to your best life with your well-behaved, healthy dog.

With your dog's current behavior issues, what stage do you believe you're stuck in? What is keeping you from moving to the next stage?

_____

_____

_____

_____

In what parts of your life have you ever achieved conscious competence of your unconscious competence (stage 5)?

_____

_____

_____

_____

How can you use your experience to help you get to stage 5 with your pet-parenting?

_____

_____

_____

_____

Pet Parent Bonding Activity

We talked about bring Conscious Competence of Unconscious Competence to your dog walks. Did you know that one of the worst things you could do while on a walk is to be looking at your phone?

When you are distracted by your phone while on dog walks, you can't see what's approaching you (another dog, a skateboard, a child, or a squirrel). You also don't notice when your dog picks something up off the ground and swallows it.

Commit to putting the phone away while on walks. You *know better*, so now *do better* in this area.

CHAPTER FIVE

Squirrel! Knowing Who You Are and What You Want in a World of Distractions

"When your values are clear to you, making decisions becomes easier." –Roy E. Disney

Before you can make the best choices *for you* and your dog, you have to know *who you are* and *what you want*. It sounds simple, but for most of us, this will be the hardest part of the process. I used to make choices based on what I assumed other people would think I should do. They weren't always choices I wanted or choices that were good for me. I also frequently made a choice because it seemed like a great idea without thinking about how it affected everybody else or considering the long term effect of my decision.

Every decision you make should be filtered through your values and your goals. If you're not sure what those are, you're making decisions based on your cultural conditioning, the input of your family and friends, what you think you're supposed to do, and what you think you're supposed to want.

That's not good enough.

The beginning of this process is to think about who you are as a person and what your core values are. Is the belief system you have for yourself or what you were taught growing up what you still believe? Once you've defined those areas, you can think about different areas in your life, whether it's your pet or your work or your spouse and ask yourself if they are in alignment with what you know you believe and what you now know about yourself.

I want you to use this space and write your answers down. Don't just think about it, don't just skim. Do the exercises and write. It makes a huge difference in your results, and it declares your commitment on paper. You may surprise yourself, and that's good. Avoid justifications, the word "but" is completely against the rules, and dig deep. The thoughts at the surface are often preoccupied with our real obligations in the moment. "I believe in _____, but _____," negates the whole thing. Don't think or edit; just write.

What are your core values? These rarely change as you go through your life. What do you believe in? This can be spiritual or just your convictions. What is true, what is good, what is real and valuable?

_____

_____

_____

_____

_____

_____

_____

What makes you angry? About other people, about yourself, about the world we live in. What pisses you off enough that you'd like to do something about it?

_____

_____

_____

What kind of pet parent are you now, and what kind of pet parent do you want to be? How do they differ?

_____

_____

_____

_____

If you have kids, what kind of parent are you now, and what kind of parent do you want to be? How do they differ?

_____

_____

_____

_____

What kind of partner are you now, and what kind of partner do you want to be? How do they differ?

_____

_____

_____

_____

What kind of employee/entrepreneur are you now, and what kind of employee/entrepreneur do you want to be? How do they differ?

_____

_____

_____

_____

Before we talk about what you want, I'd like you to look over your answers to the last questions. When you look at your core values, does your relationship with your dog align with them? Do the choices you make as pet parent seem to fit with what you believe? For example, if you hold kindness and compassion as a core value, does your dog's behavior drive you to react in unkind ways? Is it only your dog who sees it, or are you modeling it for your kids? How about the way you live your life? Are your relationships in alignment with your values? How about your career and job? If freedom and a strong family are core values for you, do your working hours reflect it?

For some of us, especially those of us who have said yes to obligation after obligation without considering our values, the gap between our deeply held values and the life we're living can be enormous. It's important not to be discouraged. This is hard work, often emotional work, but it's the work we need to do to make the kinds of changes that will make your life and your dog's life infinitely better.

When you're establishing this vision for yourself—the real you beneath all the layers of obligation, conditioning, and commitment traps—it's almost impossible to fully realize how good it can be when you're committed, motivated, and working toward the right goal. The life you want and your ability to achieve it is often not even in your realm of possibility. It's so difficult to imagine really living your purpose because *so few people do it*.

It's okay if it's hard. It's okay if it feels impossible now. I promise it's worth it.

How Do You Know What You Want?

How do you know when there's no input from anyone else – when you're the only one in the room – what you really want?

I spent years just going through the motions. I lived based on the decisions I had made (or decisions I felt were made for me), reacting to everything that came up. I was living life on life's terms, not on *my terms*. Once I became aware of how unhappy I was, I had a revelation. *There's got to be more out there than this.* And there is.

Realizing there was actually *so much more* out there, I did my own kind of soul searching and discovered I could never even try for a better life if I didn't know what it was I wanted. When I asked myself *what do you want?* I couldn't answer it.

It was astonishing I couldn't even answer what I wanted. Can you?

Of course, the negative self-talk started in: *well, how do you not know what you want? It's your life.* (Or is it?) I had spent so much time just existing—keeping up with the day-to-day stuff—that *wanting something more* seemed far-fetched and unattainable. I realized I had stopped thinking these things were possible.

Coming to terms with what you want can be a frightening thing. First, when you set a goal, you're making a commitment to it. Now you've said it, you actually need to do the work to *make it happen*. It's another item for your to-do list.

When you know what you want, you have to admit where you're falling short. You have to admit where you've let things slide for convenience or due to distraction. You've made choices to bring you to this point that didn't align with your values, and in many cases, you didn't value yourself enough to even figure out what your values were.

When you do these exercises, let go of assumptions. Assume nothing. Pretend you are a blank slate, and you've made no plans from here on out. The entire world is open to you. Maybe you always thought you wanted children – or always assumed you'd have children. When it comes down to deciding if you want children or not in your life, once you *actually think about it*, you could say "I don't know, I kind of like my life the way it is...do I want children?" Whatever you decide is fine, as long as you actually *decide*. The decision is yours, not your family's, not your culture's, and not the you from fifteen years ago. Be authentic and audacious.

What does your best life look like?

_____

_____

_____

_____

_____

_____

_____

What's your motivation for having this vision for yourself?

_____

What choices have you made in your life that have kept you from this?

_____

_____

_____

_____

Say It Out Loud

Your goals are not meant to exist in secret. It's natural for us to be a little cagey and hope everybody just notices one day we sure got awesome all of a sudden, or our dog just transformed from the Tasmanian Devil to Lassie, but when we speak it from day one, we are more successful. Stating the goal publicly and getting your support system in place is a key part of making it work.

Your support system will help you hold yourself accountable. Find people who will lift you up, believe in you, and encourage you. You may have somebody in your life who will criticize you or even make fun of you (insisting they're laughing *with* you)—"Why are you even wasting your time doing that? It's never going to change. That won't work. That's too audacious."

We already have those demons in our own head telling us lies; we don't need to hear it from somebody else. You might be wrong with the person you pick to tell. If they don't support you, it often means something about you living your best life is a little scary to them. *It probably means you're doing something right.* Maybe they're not in alignment with their own values or they're afraid you're going to leave them behind. It's never *ever* about *you*. If you do reach out and you get something back you're not expecting, know you're probably on the right track and find another person to lift you up and don't let it derail you. (Excuses. Don't go there.)

The key to your best support system is finding the *right* group of people. For your dog, a group training class is a wonderful way to stay accountable and meet people who can help you succeed and lift you up when your success doesn't come as quickly or as easily as you'd hoped. Even though everyone wants to show off the skills they worked on with their dog and how good their dog's behaving, you know you're going to get to the class and find other dog owners who can relate when you're struggling, too. Sharing in the experience with others who have similar goals is indispensable.

When I was a new dog owner, I took Tyson to a very large puppy class with about 20 other dogs and double the pet parents. This was before I had followed my current career path, so I didn't know it was way too big of a class. (With dog training, I now recommend class sizes of about 5 dogs—you get more one on one time with the trainer, and they can get to know your dog).

We were a few classes in, and they asked if anyone would like to come up to the middle to demonstrate the homework we'd been working on. I jumped up to volunteer, so excited to show off how hard we'd been working towards our goal.

We went up to the front, surrounded by these 40-60 other dogs and their owners. As we were about to start, Tyson took a huge dump right there in the middle of the floor. He was a big, 5olb puppy, and it was *huge*. It smelled awful, everyone was laughing, and I was *mortified*. I felt like the kid in grade school who stood up to give a presentation and peed his pants.

Of course, I didn't have anything on me to pick it up, so the instructor said, "Just keep going and one of the other instructors will come clean it up." Did I show my best skills that day? Not exactly. But I still came back the next week. It was embarrassing, but it didn't stop me because I didn't use it as an excuse to quit. It was a great conversation piece for the rest of the class to come up and talk to me. I got to meet people, everyone felt comfortable with me from that moment on, and I knew I could count on this group to be supportive when Tyson and I needed it.

In your non-pet life, you need the same kind of support. It's huge to find support *in the right places*. It can't just be an announce it to Facebook kind of support, where you hope the right people like it and check up on you.

If you're ready to commit to a goal, find a group of like-minded people who will challenge you, support you, and hold you accountable. When you're all working on similar goals, a group will empower you when you need motivation, lift you up when you take a faltering step, and celebrate your successes when you reach your goals or achieve smaller steps on the way to the big kahuna. On the flip side, you can do the same for them, and strangely enough, that's going to be just as good for you and keep you motivated.

A Last Word on the Pivot

Sometimes, even the right choices are not going to feel great – they'll feel right, but not great. In the past I struggled with sad feelings about being lonely. I had to realize the choice I made was the right one, and what I chose to do about it was in my control. I made the choice to get divorced (the right choice), and I could either sit around feeling sad and lonely or I could choose to remember the sense of freedom I'd given myself. I could choose to find somebody I wanted to be *not lonely* with, and continue living the life I wanted to live.

Conversely, even now after you've determined who you are and what you want, the choices we make toward our goal and with those values in mind will not always be the right ones. We are going to misstep, we are going to go one way and find out it wasn't where we should be. It's a natural part of the process.

A lot of people believe it's failure to change course or *pivot*, but there is nothing further from the truth. Don't think of it as not succeeding at a choice you make, but rather redirecting to a more beneficial and goal-oriented direction.

One caveat: when you take responsibility for another living creature then you've committed to something that needs to be seen through. A pivot doesn't mean abandoning the goal or the pet or saying, "Well that didn't work, I'm going to give up." It could mean redirecting your focus from enabling to training.

It works the same with your career, family, and life. Pivoting doesn't necessarily mean divorce. It could, but it could also mean taking a good look at your marriage, and if it's the right thing for you, focusing your energy there. Remember, two adult humans can go forth and make lives for themselves divorced, but a dog is entirely different.

Go back and take a look at your list of shiny objects. Which should you focus your energies on, and which should you pivot from? Why?

_____

_____

_____

_____

Take a look at the choices you didn't plan for. Which should you focus your energies on? Which should you pivot from?

_____

_____

_____

Who makes up your support system? How will you communicate your goals—pet and life-related—to them?

_____

_____

_____

What is the biggest aspect of your pet parenting that has to change to accommodate your values and your goals?

_____

_____

_____

Pet Parent Bonding Activity

Review what you wrote for your vision as a pet parent.
Concentrate on the things you can start doing right away to
move towards your goal without having to wait for a behaviorist
or a training class to start.

It can be as simple as committing to doing what's in their best
interest…like not feeding them "people food." Pick one thing to
do that's in alignment with who you want to be as a pet parent
and pick one thing that you want to stop doing that *isn't*. After
you've done it – reward yourself. You deserve treats, too!

I'm going to start:

_____

I'm going to stop:

_____

CHAPTER SIX

A Journey of A Thousand Wags Begins With a Single Tail

"People often say that motivation doesn't last. Well, neither does bathing - that's why we recommend it daily." –Zig Ziglar

The key to getting started is *getting started.*

No, that wasn't a typo.

I'd love to tell you once you figure out who you are and what you want, a magical yellow brick road appears before you leading you straight to the wizard, but it doesn't work like that. Even Dorothy had to decide her desire to go home was stronger than her desire to live like a queen in Munchkinland. Her desire to go home was stronger than her fear of all the obstacles she faced on the way. And like Dorothy, I can say with complete honesty that I am where I am right now because my dogs made the journey with me.

A few years had passed since we last checked in on Guinness and Clover. We had moved to the suburbs, bought a big house with a huge yard, and they transitioned pretty well. When Jimmy got his new job in New York, I didn't want to be living in a big suburban house an hour away from my businesses on my own, so we moved back into the city, Guinness, Clover, and I.

It was, of course, difficult to find a place that allowed not one, but *two* 60lb dogs, but I kept looking and found a place with an exorbitant, non-refundable security deposit, but we made it work. I made sure it had a big yard they could run around in, which was wonderful for the city.

During this time of constant transitions—from city to suburb to city, from living with my husband to living half a continent away, from struggling business owner to struggling business owner who discovers $40,000 missing—I realized I was in a place I never meant to be, and it was sucking the life out of me. It was around this same time I finally admitted I was extremely unhappy in my marriage.

It had gotten very uncomfortable to be where I was.

I forced myself to put one foot in front of the other and determine who I really was and what I really wanted (so I speak with some authority when I say I understand how difficult the last chapter can be, but I know how much you will get out of finding clarity—consider it my tough love). I evaluated where I needed to change, and where I needed to focus my energies. I decided that staying where I was and who I was sucked more than the effort it would take to change. I decided I was tired of being a dog professional with dogs who didn't listen. I needed to do *something*.

I started working with Guinness and Clover.

The dogs were my only constant. They were there for me and became my common thread when everything else in my life was in upheaval and flux. Once I started working with the dogs, I realized just by me becoming more consistent, me using the common language they understood, me being disciplined with all of the techniques, they were responding in a positive manner. Things were changing; *things were getting better*.

I looked at that and thought, "Well, gosh! If I can control this scenario I felt so hopeless in, what other areas of my life can I start to get control over?" I had been very unhappy with my marriage, and after Jimmy moved to New York it was impossible to deny the deeper issues in our relationship any longer. Seeing my situation more clearly in light of the positive things happening with my dogs, I got the confidence to end my marriage and take a hard look at what was possible for me *and set out to make them happen.*

The first thing I looked at was how unhappy I was with my weight gain during the marriage and the troubles with our relationship. I had 5olbs of extra daily reminder of those sad times. It may have felt safer to me in my first steps into this life to think of it this way, but I thought, "I really should start being more active with the dogs. Maybe I'll start running with them to help Clover release some of her energy." Yes. To help Clover.

At the time, I couldn't run anywhere. I could barely get up a flight of stairs at a fast clip. But Clover needed me! So I laced up the tennis shoes, loaded up the music, and went for a run. Okay, really I went for a long walk with some running attempts interspersed throughout. I could only run a block and then I'd have to walk a block, and it'd only be for maybe 20 minutes, but I committed every day to doing it. For Clover.

Fairly quickly, actually, I was able to run about a mile, which before I couldn't even imagine. The dogs would be out of breath, mentally and physically exhausted, happy dogs. I'd have the oxygen pumping, feel great, and remember what it was like to be a happy human.

I noticed I was losing weight and they were losing weight and everyone was feeling better. Every few days we'd add a little bit more time, and before long I was able to run 4 miles with them –about the most they could handle. I didn't stop there, though. I committed and continued running on my own or at the gym and got up to 7 miles. It was unreal! I've never been a runner, but I knew my dogs needed exercise, and by doing it together, it was our bonding time. It was not just me working out, it was time with my dogs and it was an amazing feeling.

I also started to eat better and get better food for them. They were already on a really good food, but we took it to the next level and moved to a raw diet. Everything started to improve as I focused my energies where they should be focused.

The running also gave me an opportunity to work on their training skills when we were on runs: sitting at intersections or heeling really close to me. We even reached a point where after mentally and physically exhausting Clover like she needed, she was able to play with other dogs off leash, which was not normal for her because of the level of anxiety she typically felt. Because I was able to release her stress, she could enjoy some other activities of her own that were good for all of us too.

Once I saw the unlimited potential, I started focusing energy on my business and what I *really wanted* it to be. I got finances and cash flow under control, I committed to pivoting from everything that wasn't serving my goals while planning and implementing strategies to improve things – for me, for my dogs, for my customers, for my staff, and for my community.

When I say that in 2014, I lived my best life, it is because I made my best life a priority. I put systems in place which allowed me to be the person I want to be. Not the person I think I should be or the person my parents, staff, or society thinks I should be. My business is thriving and has become an active and beloved part of my community.

And my dogs? My dogs are amazing.

Yes, it started because through my divorce and career upheaval, they were an outlet for me to put my energy into. They gave me something to commit to—a reason for getting up out of bed and getting out of depression at my worst point. But the lessons I learned changed the entire course of my life. And theirs.

They loved me no matter what I was going through and they were there for me. They created routine; they got me out of the house. If I hadn't had those dogs, I'm sure it would've been a very different experience for me than it was.

At the beginning, you have to take the first steps just because *you have to take them.* You have to decide where you are now is worse than the effort it will take to get you where you want to be. Even if you don't really think so. Even if you're comfortable in the discomfort. You have to move those feet.

Once you do get going, your motivation springs forth from your successes. It shines through the places where you fail (because you will, and that's good). It is self-generating; you just need to feed it occasionally with your effort and your well-deserved celebration of all the forward motion you make.

What obstacles do you expect to face on your journey to a well-behaved dog?

_____

_____

_____

_____

What obstacles do you expect to face on your journey to your best life?

_____

_____

_____

_____

What small change can you start with in your dog's behavior? Take a look at your dog behavior obstacles and decide which would be easier to deal with than staying where you are. Which is it? Why?

_____

_____

_____

_____

What small change can you start with in your own life? Take a look at your best life obstacles and decide which would be easier to deal with than staying where you are. Which is it? Why?

_____

_____

_____

_____

Get Control of Your Inner Dog

Listen, I know this is hard to admit, but you've got a real problem. The dog inside of you is barking so loud and so often that nobody can concentrate, least of all you. Before you do any of this, you *must* get your inner dog under control.

It's your "You can't do that," brain, and it's a beast. It yips at every action you take with an incessant stream of "Why are you even trying? That's scary! Just stay where you are, at least you have a family or a job or an income or a house." It's probably been growling since you've started reading this book, feeling like I'm invading its space and about to tell you to do something it doesn't like. And it's even angrier to discover you're listening.

How do you bring your inner dog to heel?

Acknowledge it. Know that as annoying as the barking is, your inner dog is trying to keep you safe. It is all of your caution and all of your fear wrapped up in a neat little furry package. Yours may be a Chihuahua or it may be a bulldog, but it's there. And it's loud. *And it's not going away.*

I'm not going to tell you to muzzle it, because that's pretty cruel when its intentions are good. You need to take control, choose to train it, and make it learn to listen to your commands. It can be your companion and your support *if you teach it how.*

When those thoughts come up in their yips or deep growls, thank your mental canine for its service in protecting you. Acknowledge the fear and uncertainty it's expressing. Give it a pat.

And then put it in its crate and walk away.

You can choose to listen to your instincts and cower when it barks, or you can choose to acknowledge the barking and put it aside. You can't control your fears or your feelings, you can only control how you react to them. It takes practice and commitment, but your inner dog is trainable. Start today, and watch what happens as you focus on improving its behavior.

Acknowledge your inner dog. What barks are coming to the surface as you begin the process of changing your dog's behavior and your life? What is your inner dog protecting you from? How realistic are those fears? How will you choose to react (or not) to them?

_____

_____

_____

_____

_____

_____

Your Dog Can Fetch Your Motivation

Yes! You want to live your best life. You've seen it – you wrote it down in the last chapter, you know it's possible, you know you're worth it – but your forward motion is just not happening.

If you're playing hide and seek with your motivation, start with your dog. You picked up this book to help get you out of the situation you found yourself in. You can look at the sweet face of the companion who loves you unconditionally and depends on you for his every need. I know you're a dogaholic like me, so start there.

Is the issue behavioral? Sign up for a training class today, and start building motivation and momentum as you connect with others and all see positive results with your dogs. I don't care if your dog is old or a rescue or lazy (or if you are old, a rescue, or lazy), just sign up now before you give yourself a chance to over think it.

Group dog training classes happen in almost every community around the country. Check with your local pet stores for more information. If you live in Chicago, I invite you to attend one of our training classes at Dogaholics. Sessions, descriptions, and class dates are posted at www.dogaholics.com/training.

If you'd prefer to learn from the comfort of your own home, I have a variety of training videos and guides to fit your needs at www.ultimatepetparent.com.

Could your dog use a boost in health? It's an easy fix to make in your home starting today, and will absolutely lead you down the path to changing so much more than just your pet's health.

A recent study by the Association for Pet Obesity Prevention found the 52.5% of dogs are overweight – that's 43.7 million dogs in the United States alone! *People* make this happen (because *people* are buying the food and filling the bowls) by feeding dogs an empty carb diet and frequently overfeeding them for their age and activity. It's easy to do if you follow the directions on the bag (often the only part of the bag people read – when was the last time you looked at ingredients?). Well-meaning pet owners also tend to choose terrible treats and overdo them, while not giving the dogs the kind of exercise they need.

How do you start?

Switch to high protein and low to no carb food. Pay attention to the recommended serving portions on the back of the bag, but always take into consideration the age and activity level of your pet. You can use this website to calculate how much you should be feeding your dog. Also, remember you want to be feeding the amount for his ideal weight, not his actual weight. www.dogfoodadvisor.com/dog-feeding-tips/dog-food-calculator/

Ditch the so called "diet food," even if your dog is already obese. Feed an appropriate amount of highly nutritious food, get in a higher level of daily activities, and do not feed your pet people food. You'll begin to see results, and your dog will feel so much better. Remember, one pound to a dog is practically equivalent to 20 human pounds!

Build some accountability into your plan by going public. Let people cheer on you and your dog. Get walking and build up your time and distance at intervals that feel good for your dog. Weigh in monthly and remember it's not a celebrity skinny-quick diet. Slow and steady progress for your dog is wonderful.

Reward them for their progress, but ditch the carb treats (no potato, no rice), and choose a healthier, nutrient dense treat. And remember, rewards are not just food! Reward him with extra bonding time with you. Get down on the floor and play. Your dog has a strong desire to work and to please you. He wants to be your best friend, and he wants to feel valued. You will notice not only your dog's weight and stress decreasing, but yours will decrease right along with his.

What will you do with your newfound motivation?

Pet Parent Bonding Activity

Go to the kitchen, grab your dog's bag of food, and look at the ingredient label.

If the first ingredient is something like poultry or fish, instead of a named protein like chicken or salmon (...or worse yet, if meat isn't even listed as the first ingredient), then head to your nearest local independent pet retailer and talk to them about more nutritional and biologically appropriate foods available to you.

This one, simple action will likely improve or heal most health issues they are facing AND extend their life. Knowing that should be motivation enough for you to commit to giving them food to help them thrive.

Part Three:

Live Like Every Day is Dog Park Day

Walk the Dog; Don't Let the Dog Walk You

*"Do not go where the path may lead, go instead where there is no path
and leave a trail."* -Ralph Waldo Emerson

Sure, you know who you are. Yes, you've figured out what you want. You're aware and on guard for all the traps you've fallen into, and you're ready to avoid them on the path to your goals.

It may not be paved with yellow brick, but in this section, I'm going to map out your path in front of you. You'll have to build it as you go, but once you do, you can use it again and again. Just think of it like a real life logic puzzle: you're the farmer who has to get the grain, the fox, and the hen across the river in your rowboat. You may not be able to get all of them over together, but with a little planning and commitment, you'll all end up on the other side and on the way to market. And the part of the story you never hear? The farmer killed it at the market, bought himself a boat with more seats, and his life is so much easier and more fulfilling now that he's not rowing back and forth all day.

These strategies will work whether you're tackling issues with your dog or issues in your own life. The chaos can't survive when confronted with strategy and commitment. However, even if you feel like you could take on the world right now, don't skip the chapter on managing setbacks. You will have them. They're good for you. You can choose to let them derail you or let them teach you something about yourself, your goal, or your dog.

You can control your life or your life can control you. Depending on whether you like holding the leash or sniffing the ground, how you move forward, keep your commitments, and choose your life will dictate if you are the walker or the walked.

Let's dig in and give you the tools to make this a great walk.

CHAPTER SEVEN

Set Your Leash Laws: Strategy and Boundaries

"Daring to set boundaries is about having the courage to love ourselves, even when we risk disappointing others." –Brene Brown

There are seven steps to get you where you want to go. Whether it's your dog's behavior or your own life goals, once you know who you are and what you want, *getting there* looks the same. I'll cover the first three steps in this chapter:

1. **Do Your Homework**
2. **Make Your Plan**
3. **Set Clear Boundaries**

Assuming you've never been to this magical destination of *well-behaved dog* or *your best life*, or it's been awhile since you visited, the first step is critical for your future success. It can be the trickiest, stickiest step, but you can't ever expect to achieve your goals for you or your goals for your dog without it. Let me show you why.

Do Your Homework

Before you can make any decisions or formulate a plan, you have to do your research. This step—either skipping it or deciding to live here—is why the vast majority of people never achieve their goals, settle for less, and give up on their dog and the idea of a *best life*. Truly, it's one of those make or break moments, but it's sitting quietly and unobtrusively over there in the library or behind the Google doodle of the day.

First, focus your research on the root cause of the problem, not the symptom. If your dog is barking, the problem is not the barking. The problem is what *causes* the barking. Is it separation anxiety, agitation, lack of socialization, over-protectiveness? With my dogs, when I managed my relationship with my neighbor or only went out when she wasn't home, I wasn't addressing the actual issue, just the symptoms. Nothing changed.

Your research will also help make sure your goal is S.M.A.R.T.—Specific, Measurable, Attainable, Relevant, and Timely.

You've decided what you want, but you need to decide how it really looks in practice. *I want a better-behaved dog* or *I want to be a better pet parent* are too nebulous, so if that's where you are, get very **specific.** What kind of relationship do you want to have with your dog? What levels of training do you want? Do you want to take your dog through agility competitions? Would you like your dog to be a service dog and go to nursing homes? Or would you rather he just be able to go on a walk through the neighborhood and not eat everything he sees on the ground? Would you want him to stop jumping on people?

If you decide you'd like your dog to stop jumping on people, you can **measure** your success easily. After completing the goal, is he jumping? No? Success. If you'd like your sweet-tempered dog to go to nursing homes, you can measure success with the completion of her Canine Good Citizen Certificate. "Better" is not a good yardstick, because it could mean anything from a centimeter to a foot.

Once you decide what success looks like, you begin your research. This will tell you just how **attainable** your goal is. What kind of experts are in your area? Do they have philosophies aligned with your own? What classes do they have available? What is the path it would take to get from where you are to where you want to be? What does this commitment cost in time and money? What has been the experience of others who have traveled the path ahead of you?

You've written out what your best life would look like, and what you really want from your relationship with your dog in an earlier chapter. You've figured out what you believe in, what you stand for, and exactly who you are. Use these to measure how **relevant** your goal is to the life you want to lead. If your best life includes more fresh air and a healthier life, teaching your dog to be an excellent leash-walker fits well with your values. If your values include service to others, your dog becoming certified to bring joy to nursing homes and children's hospitals would be relevant to the way you want to live your best life and worth the commitment it would take to get there.

When you know the process, you can check in on whether your goal is **timely.** If the Canine Good Citizen test seems to be about two years off for your dog, you can set smaller, specific goals between now and then. Spending two years doggedly chasing a far-off goal is a set-up for failure. We need smaller, more attainable goals along the way so we can keep up our momentum and motivation while working toward a larger goal.

Take a week, block out time on the calendar, and get this homework done. Consider it a prerequisite for the great things to follow. When the week is done, you must move on to the next step. Any less time and you run the risk of jumping into a plan that doesn't get you to your end goal because it was the path with the brightest lights or the biggest neon signs. More time, and you may never leave. It's all too easy to get stuck in the research phase trying to figure out the perfect way to get where you want to go. Staying here gives you the good feeling of having set a goal, the illusion of moving forward on it (because you're researching!), but never actually allowing you to achieve anything but a fall into those traps we talked about earlier.

We're so fortunate in the internet age to have the majority of human knowledge and experience at the touch of a button, wherever we are, whenever we feel inclined to access it. With a quick search of YouTube, you can fix your refrigerator, rewire your toaster to play mp3's, and learn to assist at the birth of a baby goat. Truly, the research potential is limitless without you ever having to get up off of your couch.

Once you start looking, you will find more shiny objects than you can count to research, but you have to set a specific time limit and move along, no matter what comes up. Trust you are a capable, self-aware adult, and a week of research is sufficient. Of course, you'll learn more along the way. For our purposes, a week of research is plenty to get you to step two.

Set a timer—your phone, the microwave—for 5 minutes. Think of all of your current commitments and put them into one of three categories: required, what you enjoy, and what's holding you back.

Required

_____

_____

_____

_____

_____

_____

_____

_____

What You Enjoy

_____

_____

_____

_____

_____

_____

What's Holding You Back

_____

_____

_____

_____

_____

_____

When the 5 minutes are up, think about each required commitment and rate yourself on a scale of 1-10 based on how well you feel like you handle each of them.

Look at your full list of commitments and choose one that would move your life forward the most if you tackled just the one thing. Do your research and make a plan for it.

Make Your Plan

I used to spend a lot of my life coming up with goals and then doing whatever I could every day to move toward them. Somehow I would accomplish many of them, but I always had more goals tacked on and no plan to speak of. I would move forward in some sense, but it was a constant rolling ball of goals—more piling up, the picture getting bigger and bigger, until it was overwhelming and knocked me over.

Make your plan by starting with your end goal. You know from your research approximately how long it takes to achieve. Set yourself a reasonable time line and put it on the calendar. From there, you work backward. I'm going to use a year as an example because it divides nice and evenly, but whatever your length of time, the process is the same.

Start with your large 1-year goal. How do you want your life to look in one year? Or less broadly: what one thing to you want to have changed one year from now? What do you need to achieve in the next quarter to make your goal a reality? Maybe it's three separate training classes and a one-on-one intensive with a trainer. Put those on the calendar and block off the time to commit to them. Determine how you will measure success. Here I'd measure success by the completion of each class and the intensive, culminating in achieving the complete goal.

Next, ask yourself what you need to do each month to meet the quarterly goal. Let's say that's attend each class session, complete all homework, and practice the skills you've learned. In order to do it, you need to arrange your other commitments to ensure you'll never have to miss a class, as well as set aside specific time to finish your homework and have one-on-one practice time with your dog. You may want to measure success by looking at the specific skills your dog will acquire during the month or the new things you are able to do with him.

Then, ask yourself what you need to do each week to meet the monthly goal. In this example, you may want to fill in your weekly planner with the specific times and days of classes as well as the appointments you've set for yourself to complete homework and practice time. You can do this every week or once a month, but make sure you do it. Your calendar will only work if you *use it*. Measure success in this example at the end of each week by how far you progressed on the skill you learned in that week's class. Are you finding it easier to integrate new skills?

Next—and this is probably the most important step in the planning process—ask yourself what you can do each day to meet your weekly goal. When you put things on your calendar, on the day-to-day level, you must block out the time and actually do them. You can think about things all day, plan for every contingency, but if you're not prepared when distractions hit, you won't get it done.

Create a morning routine for yourself to get focused on achieving your goals and living your own agenda. Brendon Burchard is spot-on when he says your inbox is like being digitally rufied. If the first thing you do in the morning is hop on your phone or your computer and check your email, you get sucked into what everyone else's agenda is, you get on everyone else's time frame for you, and it's almost impossible to go from there and set *your own* agenda. When the first thing you do when you wake up is focus on your plan (and probably your dog), your day remains in your control, even when the inbox comes into play.

With our clients at Dogaholics in our training classes, we usually set small goals. Usually the trainers work with clients in 6-week chunks. They lay out what they're going to work on so there's a clear progression from skill to skill, and you and your dog meet the deadline and small goal before you move to the next one. If you want to reach the end goal, you have to accomplish these little hurdles in between.

No matter what, I recommend spending at least 15 minutes per day working with your dog on your goals for his behavior. Not including when you work on it during walks, playtime, or bonding time, but a specific appointment to focus on things like sit stays, no barking while you're tempting them to bark, or whatever you're working on to get to your end goal for the week. When you accomplish it, you should celebrate your success and move to the next goal.

This example of a yearly goal down to the daily actions is how I recommend you address your dog's behavior, but you can use this same system to tackle anything in your life that isn't where you want it to be. Let me give you another example.

I'm on the board of Chicago Canine Rescue, and I plan their largest fundraiser, the Mutt Strut. It takes months of planning and work, but it routinely raises between $50-70,000 per year for the charity. It's an enormous project, but one with an end goal that changes the lives of so many dogs in the Chicago area. It's a *best life goal*, and one I'm thrilled to work on every year.

I begin by setting my large, long-term goal. I create a monthly, weekly, and daily plan with several smaller deadlines interspersed throughout for me to use to measure my progress, keep on track, and provide accountability. The smaller goals also create a sense of accomplishment both for me and for the team of people I enlist to make it happen. When we reach the end and the event goes off without a hitch, it's the culmination of not just one effort, but of numerous smaller steps we accomplished along the way. Even when the large goal seems far away, and sometimes nearly impossible, the smaller goals allow me to build to the end goal naturally. When I trust the plan, I get where I'm going and the Rescue gets a big check.

What is your end goal? How long will it take you to complete?

_____

_____

_____

_____

What will you do this month to reach your end goal?

_____

_____

_____

_____

What will you do this week to reach your end goal?

_____

_____

_____

_____

Set Clear Boundaries

"No" isn't just for correcting bad dog behavior. I want you to learn to love "no." Find new ways of saying it: "I wish I could, but I can't," "Nope," "Not a chance," "Ain't gonna happen." You get the picture.

Use your values to set boundaries you can stick to. You have a goal and you have a plan; now you have a reason (not an excuse) to be discerning in what obligations you take on. What's important to you? Make your choices based on what best serves your goals rather than obligation, habit, or the expectations of others.

Boundaries are crucial for your dog, as well. Clover was always a barker. She would often come into the office with me, and anytime an employee would come down the steps, Clover would bark at them to warn me they were coming. It would startle a lot of people, especially because she was pretty aggressive about it sometimes. She would never hurt them, but it was certainly annoying to them. It got to the point where one of my managers had to pull me aside and say, "You know, Candace, it seems like your dogs are barking a little bit too much. Is there anything you could do to help that?" It was a huge wakeup call telling me I needed to set some clear boundaries with Clover and do the work of teaching her to stop barking.

I hired a dog trainer and we started working every week. We would have private lessons once or twice a week, and then I'd go to a group leash-walking class to work on Clover's issues. Of course, because I had two dogs, Guinness had to fall in line as well. It came down to being consistent, always having treats around, and creating boundaries.

I started working with them on simple techniques like "place," which is where you put a mat or a bed in the room and they have to "place" and stay on their mat. They can't get off of it until you've allowed them to, and they actually can't make any noise while on place. They need to behave properly while they're on their mat, and you reward them with treats when they are behaving appropriately. To release them, you use the command "free," and you can give them treats again.

After I implemented a clear boundary in my office and home environment it was amazing at how the barking stopped when people were around because I was in control. Imagine if you were in control of your own life...what other barking would stop?

How will you change your daily routine to keep your focus on your goals and your priorities?

_____

_____

_____

_____

Describe your new morning routine, and remind yourself how it will change the way you experience your entire day. How will this help you achieve your goals and live according to your values?

_____

_____

_____

_____

Take a look at your list of what's holding you back. Which of these commitments can you pivot from? Which can you adjust so they can be placed in the "enjoy" column?

_____

_____

_____

Pet Parent Bonding Activity

I've put together a list of easy steps to be the best parent you can be. These activities are often overlooked, but are crucial to your dog's well-being. Just like changing the batteries in your smoke alarm, your dog needs "maintenance" you may only appreciate after you need it.

Your Yearly Road Map to Being an Amazing Pet Parent

Yearly
- Schedule an annual physical exam with your veterinarian to cover health, vaccines, parasites, dental health, weight and nutrition.
- Consider pet insurance or renew your policy.
- Ensure microchip information is up to date.
- Follow your area guidelines for pet registration laws.

Quarterly
- Check their ID Tags to ensure the # isn't faded and all contact information is correct.
- Take a training or agility class. Even well behaved dogs enjoy this one on one time to learn and make you proud.

Monthly

- Schedule a professional grooming or give them a bath
- Buy a new bag of food if you haven't in a month. Do not buy huge value bags that sit open and get stale.
- Wash their bedding.

Weekly

- Brush their coats using a de-shedding or de-matting brush
- Brush their teeth and gums
- Rotate your dog's toys by putting only 4 out at time. Rotate weekly to keep them engaged.

Daily

- Keep feeding and potty times consistent. Don't just leave food out. Make sure to refill or change their water.
- 1-2 longer periods of extended exercise like a walk, run, off-leash play, or game of fetch is great.
- 15 minutes of focused play or training with you
- Check the quality of their stool. It will tell you a lot about how they're feeling.
- Be consistent with commands and enforce all training rules.

CHAPTER EIGHT

Bark Effectively: Communication and Creativity

"I used to look at Smokey and think, "If you were a little smarter you could tell me what you were thinking," and he'd look at me like he was saying, "If you were a little smarter, I wouldn't have to." –Fred Jungclaus

Your dog could be barking the canine equivalent of Great Expectations, and you would never know. You'd pat him on the head, tell him shhh, and when he hunkered down quiet in his bed, you'd think he looked so cute. Meanwhile, his cute look was actually irritation at you for interrupting him just before he could close chapter 12.

The next two steps on your path to achieving your goal – with your dog or in your life – are:

4. **Communicate Effectively**
5. **Be Creative**

Without them, you run the risk of your great masterpiece never being heard or understood. And I'll give you a hint: if you don't understand your doggy Dickens, he's not going to understand you unless you enlist the help of communication and creativity.

Communicate Effectively

Your dog wants to please you. The first step in getting her on board with your behavior goals for her is to learn how to communicate with her in a way she'll understand and respond to. As humans, we are very verbal. We love our words, and we love hearing ourselves talk. Not only does your dog not appreciate your dramatic monologues, he doesn't even understand he's supposed to be listening unless you help him along. Instead of bringing him to your level, you need to be comfortable at his.

First, establish yourself as the alpha dog. Your dog needs to understand you're in charge, and she should be listening to you. Instinct will tell her since you are the alpha, she *must* listen to you. To show your dog who is really in the leadership role:

- Require your dog to do something before you give her food, water, toys, or affection. This way she earns her reward. For example, have her sit before each of these activities.
- Always walk out the door ahead of your dog when going through doorways. Have your dog sit before you open the door. After you walk through first and call her through, have her sit again on the opposite side of the door while you close and lock up.
- During walks, do not allow your dog to walk in front of you or pull you down the street. Instead, keep your dog to your side as much as possible. Use a 6-foot leash. Retractable leashes create bad behaviors and show your dog he has whatever freedom he wants. This is counteractive to establishing you as pack leader.

You *can* learn to speak dog fluently. Understand first and foremost that you and your dog communicate with each other all the time – without any words at all. The type of energy you are holding, your dog is picking up on it. Your dog doesn't understand the complexity of human emotions. Remember, you've got the higher order thinking skills in this relationship, and he instinctively picks up on your demeanor. If you're calm, your dog feels calm and secure knowing you are in control. If you lose control of your emotions or carry stress, anxiety, or anger, your dog senses you are out of control and he goes into danger-mode. He can't keep himself under control if you can't keep yourself under control.

If you want to change his behavior, you have to change yourself as well. It's critical to remember you can choose how much stress you carry. You can understand the ramifications of your choices and adapt to them. Your dog doesn't get to make that choice, you make it for him. And no matter how much stress you think you can handle, trying to find your limit is never a good thing for you, either.

Learning this skill with your dog will help you in other situations, as well. The energy you're putting out is picked up by the people in your life, though they may not be as efficient as your dog in their immediate response to it. I know my team can sense when I am stressed out and pick up my energy. The entire workplace feeling changes. If you're a parent and you're short or stressed or upset, your kids will pick up on it, and those are the skills you're teaching them on how to react to situations.

Since communication is a two-way street, learn how your dog is communicating with you. And no, that doesn't mean you have to learn to understand his newest bark-novel. Your dog communicates with his body language. Watch his tail and ears when he's feeling calm and happy. See how it changes when he's agitated or anxious.

When you do use verbal commands, make sure you're using words in a way your dog can quickly learn and understand. When I started spending time working with the trainer privately, I realized my lack of being clear or direct with Clover was causing her to not listen to me at all. Since I'm your typical talking human, my frustration that she wasn't listening made me talk *more* instead of with more clarity. Sound familiar?

I remember a nice spring day when Clover and I were out on a walk with the trainer. It was in the early stages of training, and he was encouraging me to give her specific commands to get her to listen to me. I would say, "OK, Clover, come on now! Heel, Heel! Come on, Clover, heel. Heel now,

Clover!" To her, it sounded like the adults in any Peanuts cartoon "Wah wah wah waaaaah. Wah wah wah wah." It was just *too many words*.

Even when we're using the word No, it's rarely just "No." It's "No, no, Clover! That's not right. Come on now, Clover, listen to me. I want you to come over here and I want you to heel. No! Don't do that! Stop smelling that stick. Come on, over here! Stop it! Stop it! No, no, no!" That's how I would talk to her.

The trainer said, "That's not being clear. You're not owning it." He explained, "You know, first of all, dogs hear us talk in conversation constantly so she doesn't know you're actually speaking to her. *She doesn't know she needs to listen to you.* You need to pick one word, *say it once*, and they need to listen to you. You shouldn't have to repeat yourself."

Take "no" for example. We say the word "no" so much in conversation—"Would you like another drink?" "No, that's ok." "Would you like to go do this?" "No. I don't really feel like doing that." So they hear "no" a lot in everyday language. When you want to get the *idea* of "no" across to them, it's better to use different sounds. Try a sharp "Eh. Eh." or "ssss." Whatever feels comfortable to you is fine, as long as it's something different than "no."

She began to listen to me as I said "Clover! Heel!" It's very clear, and I was telling her exactly what I wanted her to do. If she listened to me, she got treats and if she didn't, she heard "Eh. Eh." She was rewarded for the behavior I wanted to see, and she understood when she wasn't doing something I needed her to do.

Just like learning to control your own body language, you can take the principle of clarity and simplicity into anything you're trying to communicate. Whether you're communicating to your coworkers, your children, your spouse, or even yourself, (especially in pursuit of your goals), if you're not clear and specific on what you want your words can be interpreted on many different levels. Without clarity, what you get is not always what you want, and what you say is not always what you meant to express.

You set your goal for yourself and for your dog, but knowing it is not enough. You have to be specific when you create your goal, but you also need to be specific and clear when you articulate it to others. If not, no treat. Those are the rules.

This is never more evident than when you're looking for support from others as you make your journey. Especially when looking for expert help for your dog, it's critical to learn to articulate your values and communicate them (as well as read between the lines when evaluating whether a support-person is in alignment with who you are and what you want—you can't always look at the tail and ears here for clues). While most trainers are caring, kind, and committed, there are also a lot of bad trainers out there.

Anyone can teach dogs and say they're a dog trainer without a training license. This puts the burden on you to do your research and make sure you're hiring a trainer who believes in your same philosophies. I always recommend positive reinforcement – dogs (and people) respond better and more quickly to positive rather than negative. This seems fairly standard as research evolves, but there are still trainers (and "trainers") stuck in the outdated mindset of bullying the dog into submission.

We had a Dogaholics client who got a recommendation for a dog trainer elsewhere. She already had a dog who was older, and she adopted a puppy. The puppy was full of puppy energy (of course), and she was committed to integrating the new dog into her family in the best way possible for both dogs. She knew she wanted to work with a professional to help her manage this process, so she hired based on the recommendation alone.

She called me after this trainer recommended she keep her puppy living in a crate for two months while the older dog got used to a new dog being in the house. The trainer told her not to let the puppy out of the crate except for certain, short times. Basically, this dog would be spending two months of its life almost completely in a crate. She said to me, "I just think that's strange. Why would she tell me to do that? I'm now wondering if this may not be the best home for the puppy. Maybe I shouldn't have brought this puppy into my life. It's got to be better than living in a shelter, but I just can't keep the dog in a crate for two months." The lesson here extends beyond dog trainers.

If you need permission, I'm happy to give it to you. You have my official permission to listen to your instincts and trust your values are sound. Don't second guess yourself based on what an "expert" says, rather find an expert whose values align with yours. That's not to say you shouldn't work with someone who challenges you to stretch and move outside your comfort zone, nor should you look for someone who is going to tell you everything you do is great. Run far, far away when their advice conflicts with your beliefs. If your notions of right and wrong are tested by working with them, fire them!

Needless to say, I gave the same advice to my Dogaholics client. To introduce a puppy to an older dog, you have to use what you've learned about communication and allow them to "speak dog" to each other. Yes, the new dog is going to jump all over the older dog because it's a puppy. Your job is to be ready to correct the behavior, and allow the older dog to communicate to both you and the puppy. He will give off dog language and correct the puppy in a way that's appropriate and the puppy will respond. That's how puppies learn – they learn from the older dogs what's right and wrong. If it starts to become too annoying for your older dog, *then* you separate them. You can separate them with a gate; they don't need to live in crates.

As important as it is to learn how to communicate, it's equally important to learn how *not* to communicate. Study after study after study has shown that using positive reinforcement to train your dog is at least equally effective if not more effective than the older style "dominance" method. More importantly, dogs who are trained using positive reinforcement show fewer problematic behaviors (requiring less correction and training on your part), and they show fewer fearful reactions to other dogs. Every major, reputable animal organization including the ASPCA recommends the positive reinforcement method of training.

At Dogaholics, we've found with our own dogs, the dogs of our clients and customers, and all the dogs who come to our training groups, day care, and classes: dogs respond better and are more likely to learn through non-aggressive forms of communication. Positive reinforcement combined with clear and effective communication means a more successful training experience. With Clover, we used positive reinforcement—she got rewarded with a treat when she listened to me. When I became more clear and direct with how I communicated with her—simplified everything and was consistent—she learned faster and everything started to change more quickly.

While it may not be a specific directive of the ASPCA, treat yourself with the same kindness you show your dog. Negative self-talk and beating yourself up when you take a wrong step is both counter-productive and a carte blanche invitation to the chaos to show up again and wreak its havoc. When you tear yourself down, your motivation suffers, your self-worth suffers, and your commitment to your goals suffer. Now that you know *you* create the chaos in your life, don't help it gain a foothold.

These same principles apply in the rest of your day-to-day life. If you can practice it with your dog, and then with yourself, imagine the kinds of changes you can bring to the people around you. If you are more confident and *positive* in your leadership at work, imagine how you can change the culture of your workplace for the better. If you can show positive leadership to your kids, imagine the tools you're giving them when they come up against difficult things in their own lives. It all comes down to bringing consciousness to everything you do and say—because you can't take it back.

But you *can* do better next time.

Write down three negative thoughts you've had about your dog and his/her behavior. Reframe them as opportunities and write them again.

_____

_____

_____

_____

Write down three negative thoughts you've had about yourself. Reframe them as opportunities and write them again.

_____

_____

_____

_____

Where could you be clearer in your communication? What has been misunderstood or misconstrued by the listener? How can you use this clarity to get further on the path to reaching your goal?

_____

_____

_____

_____

Be Creative

Just as it's imperative for you to use your values when you're choosing how to act and who to listen to, it's important for you to trust yourself and your ability to solve problems creatively while you work with your dog and on your life goals.

Too often we want to achieve our goals by following a step by step checklist where we complete task A, move on to task B, finish up with task C, and everything wraps up and is tied with a neat little bow. If only it worked like that.

I see countless people coming in to Dogaholics—caring, loving pet parents who for whatever reason stopped trusting themselves and stopped trusting their dog. In Chapter 2, I talked about the kinds of traps people fall into, and I'll tell you now that creativity acts as a shield against some of the worst offenders: making excuses, enabling, and fear. It's okay to turn on your creative brain as you make these changes, in fact if you don't, you'll find yourself back on the train to chaos with you the one shoveling coal into the fires.

We hear a lot of excuses that enable bad behavior in dogs and bad pet parenting in people at Dogaholics (listen, guys, you know I adore each and every one of you, so know I'm telling you this with love). My dog is too lazy, my dog isn't motivated by food, my dog is too old. If you bump up against something that feels like an excuse, tap into your creative brain and think outside the box.

Your dog is too lazy or old to get enough activity, eh? Walking and dog parks are not the only activity possibilities. There are some wonderful canine swimming pools which are wonderful for dogs who may not have the joint health they did when they were younger (or slimmer). Just like all the silver sneakers folks hit up the water exercise classes at local rec centers around the country, your senior or overweight dog could benefit from a nice dip.

Nothing nearby for you? When was the last time you got down on the floor and really played with your dog? Not just a scratch on the head and a tweak of the chew toy, but consistent, sustained, active play for 10-15 minutes. Try it. And keep doing it. It's called *activity*, and it's good for you both.

Your dog isn't motivated by food, eh? Remember Clover and the squirrels? She loves chicken jerky. *Loves* it. But squirrels just seemed so much yummier. (I mean, who can blame her, the squirrels actually make you chase them – the chicken jerky just lays there.) I could have enabled the bad behavior – she's just not motivated enough by food. She can't learn to stop dragging me down the road after those squirrels. Instead, I got creative with the treats. I knew there would be something she would respond to. A bit of dried lamb lung, and those squirrels are just fluff and nothing. She can resist, and she was trainable.

If food *really isn't* a motivator for your dog, don't assume you should just throw in the towel and accept terrible behavior forever. Big sigh. Poor me. *Be creative.* I guarantee your dog is motivated by *something*. Eye contact, a round of toss the tennis ball, some bonding play time, a butt scratch. If you can't figure it out on your own, ask for help. Call Dogaholics, call your friend with the well-behaved dogs, ask the magic oracle of Google.

There are only two rules here as you're using your creative brain and the resources available to you to find solutions. First, make sure you let your values lead you when you choose from the options and you never, ever say, "Oh, that won't work," unless you've actually tried it (consistently) and it actually didn't work. Second, use the tools available to you as training aids, but beware of shiny objects. Research your choice of product, and when you purchase it, commit to learning how to use it properly and *actually using it* to get past the learning curve and truly see the opportunity for a solution to your problem. When in doubt, again, ask for help.

Your dog will respond the best to the solutions you come up with if you get your whole family and pet sitters on board. Everyone who interacts with your dog needs to know the commands. Everyone on my team learned how to lead the dogs, to put them on their place mats, and everyone needed to have the same correction words. Clear, effective communication mixed with creativity *from everyone* will change your dog (and will change your life as you gain so much more freedom to really experience life as a great pet parent).

When I realized that *Clover*, this dog who had *never* listened to me was now listening because I had become the clear authority, it triggered something in me. I realized if I got clearer and more confident in how I communicated in a lot of other areas of my life, I could surely make other positive changes. It was my lightbulb moment. I had gotten control over this thing I didn't think was possible to change, because I was making excuses. To all my wonderful customers I just called out a few moments ago for making excuses, this next story is all for you.

Before I made the commitment and got Clover's barking under control, my Dogaholics customers would often ask me, "Why isn't Clover in the store?"

I would reply, "Oh, she has issues. She needs a bandana that says *I HAVE ISSUES*. She barks at everybody like an attack dog, but really she's just saying *HEY MOM, LOOK WHO'S HERE!* She would never hurt anybody, it just comes across that way, so she has to stay home." Turns out, I'm the one who needed the *I HAVE ISSUES* bandana. Do you need one, too?

What problem have you had with your dog's behavior you thought could never change? What excuses did you make to enable the bad behavior? Take each excuse and think of three possible creative solutions.

_____

_____

_____

_____

Pet Parent Bonding Activity

Practice positive reinforcement. Work where you are with your dog, but hit up a dog store local to you for some new treats (healthy ones!). Let your dog decide which one motivates her!

Take 15 minutes today—set a timer if you need to—and get down on the floor to play with your dog. Don't *think*, just play. Watch her communication cues and see how she reacts to your playful energy.

Practice clear communication with your dog. If you're tempted to explain a concept or use lots of words, dial it back and choose one. Stick with it. Watch as your dog's demeanor changes and she really listens to you.

Next time you walk in your front door, stop for a moment and check your energy. Are you projecting calm, open, confidence? If not, shake it off and choose calm. Watch the reaction of your dog.

CHAPTER NINE

Chase It Until You Catch It: Commitment and Consistency

"Trust is built with consistency." -Lincoln Chafee

You can have the best plan in the world; your research can be impeccable, your communication clear and direct, and you can get the best start anyone has ever gotten on any plan *ever* and still fail to reach your goal. Why? Step six. Without these pieces, it's game over. Thanks for playing. They are:

6. Commitment and Consistency

and you should consider them your new best friends.

Commitment doesn't make you a good person, just like lack of commitment doesn't make you a bad one. All it signifies is this person has made a choice—either a choice to be committed or to quit. A choice to be consistent or haphazard. If you haven't been committed in the past, it doesn't mean you can't now, it just means you haven't chosen it up until now. And now you need to.

The biggest reason why commitment and motivation fail is because we do the same kind of enabling we do with our dogs to ourselves. We let ourselves off the hook when we should be accountable. We make excuses for ourselves and don't set the kind of boundaries we need to be successful. It's not a culturally popular sentiment, but we need structure as human beings as much as the dogs do. Commitment is work. It's a choice every day.

When you write your plan on the calendar, it is just that—a plan. It doesn't become who you are and how you live unless you treat it as more than words on a page. You have to invert the normal order of things – instead of spending your time putting out all the fires that come up, you have to make the plan the priority. You can delegate the fires, you can delegate tasks, but you can't delegate your life.

Making Your Commitment

Your dog is a living, breathing creature who you have chosen to join your family. Unlike your kids, unlike your in-laws (mostly), unlike your favorite auntie and uncle, you did the research and chose exactly the right dog for your family and lifestyle. Or you didn't and now you're figuring out how to make it work. You chose your dog, and everything he has, everything he does, and everything he *is* is wholly dependent on the choices you make for him. It's an enormous commitment, but it's worth it. You both deserve it.

Maybe you're at the end of your rope. You may have considered relinquishing or rehoming your dog because you don't know what to do or where to turn. Even if you've not reached that point, you may have given up on ever having the kind of life with your pet that you expected. You might just be going through the motions and *keeping him alive* without attending to his *quality of life.*

I want to tell you it's not too late to make this change. It is not shameful to *re*commit, in fact it shows great strength and courage.

The same holds true with your best life. I know the term is passed around in daytime talk shows and self-help paraphernalia enough that it starts to lose meaning. Or worse, these gurus start to tell you what it's "supposed" to mean—as if they get to choose what it should look like for you.

You get to choose based on your core values and what you really want. But just like you *must* commit to your dog, you *must* commit to your goals. The life you *really want* must be treated like a living, breathing part of you to be attended to and nurtured. Making a commitment to your best life means making it a priority and *consistently* working toward it. If you do, you'll achieve more than most people can imagine. If you don't, you'll stay stuck. The problem with stuck is now you know how unfulfilling and ridiculous those excuses holding you back are. It'll be much harder for you to remain distracted by the shiny objects now because you recognize them for what they are.

You're officially ruined for anything less than your full potential. You're welcome.

Where have you not shown your commitment to your dog? What caused you to make that choice? How would you handle it now?

_____

_____

_____

_____

Consistent Effort Produces Consistent Results

The easiest way to be consistent is to set a routine and stick with it. The goal of a routine is to bring you up the stages of competence until it's automatic for you to be working on your goal. It should feel stranger to deviate from it than to follow it daily.

When you have to deviate from your dog's training, it's critical to not simply let it slide, but rather to delegate it to another family member or professional. You learned in the last chapter how to communicate effectively, so make sure when you need someone to pick up the slack that you've given clear, accurate instructions and *they* know how to communicate those instructions to your dog.

The key to consistency is motivation, and the key to motivation is success. When we created your plan, we broke your big goal down into smaller goals that can be achieved on a shorter time frame. Work toward those individual goals and celebrate their achievement, knowing it's all bringing you closer to your best life goal. With your dog, if you had to focus on the year as a whole, working the whole time trying to reach this one, major end goal, you'd quit faster than you can say, "Squirrel!" When you see progress, you know you're not wasting your time. You have successes and achievements to celebrate with your dog (always more fun with a friend). Even as you work through this book, each chapter builds on what you've learned and will help you get to your goals.

Clover's barking problem became the neighborhood's barking problem every time we went out on a walk. Her big trigger was Wrigley Field (I am told she's not alone in this affliction, though it looked pretty good there for a while a few years ago). She would bark intensely whenever we got near it. You can understand why—there are a lot of people walking around, a lot of noise, the vendors, people screaming, and drunken revelry along with the normal ambulances and traffic on the busy street.

When I would walk her on leash through there, it would really upset her. I would tense up, she would get nervous, and I would really have to keep her close to make sure she didn't jump up on somebody. I was always nervous she would nip at a random Cubs fan (they're very sensitive about that sort of thing). The problem wasn't Clover or her barking; the problem wasn't even the Cubs fans or the extra-loud beer vendors. The problem was me.

I shouldn't have even been putting her there in such a chaotic environment because it wasn't setting her up for success. Yes, my *end goal* could be walking her through Wrigley during a Cubs game with Clover not feeling anxious or acting out. We live in the neighborhood, Clover didn't choose our house, and we both have to deal with the noise and the crowds.

If I start out walking her through mid-game craziness, I'm likely to throw in the towel and feel like it's never going to happen, might as well quit. Or move. Or teach her to use the toilet and the treadmill in the house. If instead I start with the basics and commit to making a consistent, daily effort toward smaller goals, we're more likely to reach our end goal without biting a Cubs fan.

We start week one working on getting her to have no anxiety when we're walking in a calm space. We walk four times a day, so there are plenty of chances to practice, keeping the treats handy. If there's an issue I can think creatively about how to motivate her or even consult an expert for more help. We achieve the goal and celebrate it. Progress is awesome.

Week two we walk by the coffee shop. There are people hanging around outside, there are other dogs being lazy underneath the café tables, and some days there are even a few kids hanging around with their parents. When she can handle it, we celebrate our success and move up.

Week three we walk by Wrigley Field two hours before the game. There's a little more activity, the street is busier, there are people milling around. Nobody's drunk yet (at least not much), there's no crowd to scream and cheer, the announcer is resting his voice for the big game, and the chaos is more controlled. It may take work this week. We may need to revisit the treats, and I will absolutely need to check my own posture and presence. Am I a calm, confident leader? I've seen Clover make great strides in the previous weeks, so I can come to the experience with confidence in her and the knowledge she can succeed. She knocks it out of the park, and we celebrate her success and move to the next goal.

It's only *then* when we attempt walking through Wrigley when it's full blown chaos. It's then when you can be buoyed by all of the previous successes, and this big goal that seemed so impossible at the beginning is just the next step. Not a scary step or a far-fetched step, just *the next one*. And I was always prepared with plenty of lamb lung treats. Her motivator. What's your motivator?

Here is the universal truth that Tyson and I learned early on at the ill-fated puppy class: if you start at the end goal, you're going to take a crap in the middle of the room.

Remember, the end goal doesn't have to be as monumental as Clover ready to sign up for her Canine Good Citizen test to go work at hospitals. The end goal that would *make our lives better* was just to walk through my neighborhood. I committed to her, to her health, and to her happiness. I'm incorporating her into my lifestyle because *I made the choice* to bring her into my life.

Whether your dog is 6 months old or 6 years old, she's teachable. Even if you never had any expectations for her before, even if she's lazy, even if she's a rescue. And in case you were wondering, you are teachable, too. Even if you are 35 or 47 or 62. You simply have to commit to a goal and work toward it consistently. Keep your eye on the prize. The reward just has to be strong enough – for you and for them.

What would your life look like if you made consistent effort for the next month toward the behavior you'd like to see in your dog?

_____

_____

_____

_____

What would your life look like if you made consistent effort for the next month toward your best life goal?

_____

_____

_____

_____

Option #1: Take your dog out at the same times every day. For example, take him outside the first thing in the morning when he wakes up, when you arrive home from work, and before you go to bed.

Option #2: Feed your dog on a set schedule, once or twice a day at the same time. Their bodies have an amazing internal system that prepares enzymes ahead of schedule to digest food, so when the expected food isn't presented at the right time it can cause an upset tummy. (Have they ever thrown up yellow bile? It's often because their internal clock told them it was time to eat and nothing was presented to them).

Option #3: Command consistency. Everyone in the family should use the same commands. Post these where everyone can become familiar with them. Consistency means always rewarding the desired behavior and never rewarding undesired behavior. The most commonly used commands for dogs are listed here but feel free to use your own as long as everyone is using the same ones. For example, you can't use the word "tinkle" and then your spouse use the word "potty".

"Stand," "Come," "Heel," "Leave it," "Settle," "Sit," "Stay," "Down" (means lie down), "Off" (means off of me or off the furniture)

CHAPTER TEN

When the Biscuit Crumbles: How to Roll With Setbacks

"When you feel lousy, puppy therapy is indicated." –Sara Paretsky

The last step goes hand in hand with commitment and consistency, but it's so important it gets its own chapter. Step seven is:

7. Manage Setbacks

When your commitment and consistency crap out on you, this is how you regain your motivation, restart your momentum, recommit to your goal, and get a move (back) on.

I'm not going to sugarcoat this process for you and say you *may* need this chapter. This *will happen*. Not maybe, not hopefully not. This will happen. It's what *you do* and the choices you make when it happens that determine your success. Will you actively manage the setbacks or will you let them derail your progress and send you back to square one?

Your motivation isn't going to be perfect. You're going to have moments where you misstep (in something). You are going to take a big crap in the middle of the room. It's going to happen; it's going to be part of your story. But you'll survive it, you'll move along, and you'll connect to more people. When you're living your best life—when you do this work—I promise you won't even smell it anymore.

Setbacks in the Wild

Setbacks can take many forms, but you're already ahead of almost everyone else because you know they're not an "if," they're a "when." For Clover and Guinness, it looked like mange.

You may remember we were barely into the puppy class with them when mange struck and kept them home until it cleared up. Did it have to completely derail us? Absolutely not. Did it? It sure did. I waited years before committing back to formal training for them – and that was years I spent with out of control dogs, dogs I made excuses for, dogs who limited how I could live my life. Let's do better for you.

Setbacks don't always come in the form of catastrophic system failure. The most insidious kind of setback is entropy, and half the time you don't even realize it's happening. Entropy is defined as *a gradual decline into disorder*. You start with commitment, and in your excitement it's easy to be consistent. After a few weeks you skip a day of training because you had something come up. And after all, you're walking 4 times a day, right? That has to count. A month later and you're doing the 15 minute focused training only once a week. Your dog's behavior has taken a slide, but it's not quite as bad as it once was, so you don't take action. In 6 months you forget what it felt like to have everything under control. It happened slowly, slowly, slowly until all your hard work vanishes.

Thank you, entropy. You're no longer welcome.
Where in your dog's behavior have you experienced entropy? What did you let slide that you shouldn't have?

_____

_____

_____

_____

No matter whether the setback comes as a big jolt or a slow slide, the steps to manage it are the same. The key is to recognize the setback is happening and *start the steps*. When you move through them, make sure you're always working within your core values you established in the beginning. Use them as a yardstick for all of your choices, especially the hard ones.

When Tyson was nearing the end of his life, he started having seizures from a brain tumor. We tried to make sure he was comfortable and had a great quality of life, so we kept him active and walking out in the community. The tumor affected his personality, so it was difficult knowing exactly how he would react to things – even though we were attuned to one another.

When he and I were out in the neighborhood one day, a little girl—maybe two years old—came running up to him. He's not around children very often, so I was a little wary. The mom was about 20 feet away and called over, "Oh, I just wanted her to pet the dog. She loves all the neighborhood dogs."

Now, Tyson was about 100lbs, and the little girl didn't even come up to his full leg length. It was a little disconcerting for her to be so cavalier with a strange dog, but we talked, she pet him, and he was being really good. I talked to her about how you always should ask the owner before petting a dog and to make sure the little girl lets the dog smell her hand first.

After the little girl had pet Tyson and moved along, I stepped away for a moment to go a few feet away. Tyson was staring at me, not looking at them. It all happened so fast, but felt like slow motion. The little girl came back, running up behind him, and bopped him hard on the back end. He turned, startled, and bit her right in the face.

I came running back, and I grabbed the little girl and picked her up. I immediately checked the little girl over, and I was shocked he would do something so out of character. Most of all, I was so concerned for the little girl. I apologized, and the mom said, "I'm sure it's fine," thinking the little girl just fell.

I said, "No! He *bit* her!"

The mom was horrified, concerned for her child, and initially it seemed she was most upset at herself for not supervising her daughter. She grabbed the little girl and started running.

Step One: Own It

She panicked. And in her shoes, I'm not sure I would have done any different. In all honesty, I was feeling a lot of the same panic myself.

I was freaking out first because it was horrible to see this "child of mine," the animal I loved act in a way I would never think would happen. I felt terrible for the little girl: how would she heal? Would she be afraid of dogs? Those thoughts were making me even more upset, because we were trying to have kids. *What's going to happen with him around my kids*, I thought. Would she file a police report? Would they make me put him to sleep because he had bitten someone? I had no idea what was going to happen, and I couldn't control any of it.

The *only* thing I could control were my own actions.

Since she had run away, she didn't know anything about his health or the safety of her child from preventable diseases. I immediately went home and scanned the veterinary office proof of vaccinations and wrote her a letter. I apologized greatly, gave her my contact info, and let her know I would help in any way I could. I let her know how bad I felt, and how I was willing to do whatever was necessary.

While a lot of lawyers would say I should never have done that or admitted to the problem, I choose to filter everything through my personal core values. I am responsible for my pet. Full stop.

I took the letter and walked the whole block. I saw where she ran, but I didn't know for sure which house was hers. I knocked on all the doors, rang all the doorbells, and looked for children's things. I finally got a couple of neighbors to answer the door and when I described the girl and mom they told me where she lived. They weren't home, but I left the letter.

She reached out to me later, showed me some photos, and was so glad it wasn't worse. Her reaction, instead of getting angry at me or claiming anything with Tyson was to ask me to to be more careful with him now that we knew this had happened. I said, "Yes, absolutely."

I took ownership of what had happened, and I didn't back down from this scenario. I could have easily retreated into "protect me" mode and not even acted like I was sorry. I could have made a scene and blamed the girl or the mom. I could have made it much worse based on emotions instead of *thinking about what really mattered*. What really mattered was her daughter. I wanted her to know I wasn't running away from it, because personal integrity is in line with my core values.

Your setback may not be so dramatic, but the first step is still important. If entropy has created a gap between the commitment you need to have in order to achieve your goals and what you're doing, you have to own the problem. Either you admit it and move to the next step, or you let it keep sliding until you have to start over again. Take your pick.

Step Two: Learn From It

For people who don't have dogs, it's hard to know how to act. I learned from the incident with Tyson that I could never assume people would know how to navigate a scenario with my dog. Bad experiences will sometimes happen with dogs, but you can make it go as smoothly as it can. I learned to be an advocate for my dog, and now setbacks like this are very unlikely to happen.

Just like your dog doesn't pick where they live or what they eat, you have to be your dog's voice in public. If your dog is older, if your dog is not a dog who likes to be pet, you need to scan the crowd and be aware of your surroundings and know if there are kids coming or issues that could come up.

As a committed dog owner, be ready to intervene and don't ever be afraid to speak up for your dog.

How can you be an advocate for your dog in public?

_____

_____

_____

_____

Whether you've experienced entropy or something unexpected has come up, you can learn from it and make sure it doesn't trip you up again.

If your commitment level has taken a hit and has slid down more and more as you've gotten used to each dip, take a look at your accountability measures. How are you measuring success? How are you making sure you're moving forward rather than staying still or sliding back? Are you the only one who knows about your goal enough to notice? Revisit and restructure your accountability. Find a group, create an objective measure you can use at the end of each week or month to make sure you're on track. If you start to slide again, make the measurements happen with a greater frequency.

When plans change, your dog gets mange, or you evaluate your goal and realize it's not where you really want to be, you have to pivot, adapt, and keep moving forward in the new direction. Always go back to your core values to find strength to maintain and keep going. They will never steer you wrong.

Remember a setback is simply an opportunity to hone your plan to better serve the lifestyle you want to lead and your end goal. Setbacks can sometimes tell us places in our plan where we can't sustain the kind of effort or perfection required, so we make adjustments. Often we have to adjust the plan where it lacks balance (because setbacks love to find places like that to exploit).

If you're trying to achieve a healthier pet (or a healthier you), but find there are too many instances where you're having fun and enjoying the snacks too much (or your dog is loving the treats from the excellent positive reinforcement), don't try and force yourself to fall back in line and avoid them altogether. Balance the treats with more exercise.

If you find you're laser focused on your goal without balancing it with *enjoying life*, your setbacks will show up as burnout and unhappiness. Your dog will pick up on it, and it will prevent you from reaching your goals. Remember, the journey is important. Allow room in your plans to enjoy the things that were fulfilling to you before you went off track. Before your life became an obligation rather than an adventure.

The whole reason you want a dog who behaves better or to live your best life is to reach the point where life becomes a fun adventure that you are privileged to experience. If your plan is worse than where you're leaving, you'll have a hard time finding motivation to get to your end goal. It can't all rest on where you're going – the plan should make you love where you are along the way.

Step Three: Move On

Now listen, even though the goal of this book is helping you understand *it's your fault*, it's not meant to make you feel bad or hopeless. It's meant to make you feel *powerful*. You chose this animal, and you make their choices for everything. If you make a choice that wasn't your best, you can make a different choice tomorrow. Move on.

If you want to lose weight, you made the choice of what to put in your mouth. You have total control over the choice to get up and work out or the choice to have a big pizza and a bunch of beer. You have to let go of the shame of the choices – it's not good or bad, it's just a choice you made. You can be a totally different person tomorrow. The result is completely in your control. Just own it, change it, and move on. Don't run around in circles chasing your tail and fretting about something you can't change. Take action on what you *can* change – the choices you make from now on.

I could have internalized Tyson's bite fiasco. I went over it in my mind and thought of all the things I could have done differently. I thought of all the ways I should have had more control, the ways I shouldn't have assumed someone else would pay attention. I could have let it color the way I interacted on walks with people in my neighborhood. And I did, but only in the positive. I made changes that helped my dogs and I enjoy our wonderful neighborhood safely and enjoyably rather than retreating into our house and closing all the blinds, hoping no one would notice us.

Your Dog Is Your Reset Button

Our dogs add so much value to our lives, and have true health benefits for us. They help us decrease the stress — especially the stress from this kind of setback.

I was in the midst of working on this book when I had the opportunity to go to Africa. I admit, I was a little overwhelmed trying to get it done while also running my business and getting everything in order to be out of the country for almost two weeks.

The dogs kept pestering me because they wanted to go outside. I was hitting a roadblock anyway, so I went ahead and took the dogs out. It had snowed, and I spent a lot of time enjoying them; running around; playing fetch. As we played, all these ideas started flowing. The creative ideas that had eluded me were flowing, and I felt less stressed and more centered. When I came back in, I was able to just plug away and get done what I needed to do.

Dog people are lucky. We have an automatic reset button sitting next to us wanting to go outside and play. Put this book down and go with them. Trust me.

What choices do you need to let go of and move on from? How will you make different choices in the future?

_____

_____

_____

_____

Pet Parent Bonding Activity

Read the last chapter (coming up), then put the book down, go outside, and play with your dog.

CHAPTER ELEVEN

Every Dog Will Have Its Day

"Dog lovers are a good breed, themselves." –Gladys Taber

Bad dogs are a direct reflection of lazy owners. Plain and simple. It's not the dog, it's you. But, *it's not you*, because you know better. Jump into the relationship, get committed again, and fall back in love with your dog and the wonderful life you can have as pet parent.

You have the choice to make a change or stay where you are. Your dog is counting on you to make a good one. Does this look like your house? You put the dog away when people come over (if they can even come over). Your neighbors complain of noise, or you're constantly afraid they will. You may have even been visited by the police or animal control with a barking violation.

Your dog may be obese or have health issues. Are you overweight with him? Are walks fun or a chore? Do you even take them? Can you?

Now imagine instead a calm home. Your family can enjoy each other, your dog knows her boundaries, and you can be comfortable. When guests come over, they remark about how nice your dog is, and you have the opportunity to show off a little of her training. Your dog has less anxiety when you're gone and you can enjoy your time away knowing they're comfortable and secure. Your neighbors enjoy your time away because they don't hear a peep.

You can visit the dog park, the dog beach, or Dogaholics with your dog who can romp and play appropriately with other dogs and sit quietly on leash while you make a purchase (only the purchase you meant to make, not the treat she shoplifted).

It's your choice, which life will you live?

You have all the tools you need to make amazing changes in your dog's life. As a nice added bonus, improving the well-being of your dog will have enormous repercussions for you, too.

We started by figuring out what happened to get your dog's behavior so out of whack. Your honesty is crucial. Don't be afraid to revisit this whenever issues come up.

You established a new vision for yourself, honed in on your core values, and found your motivation. You crafted a plan and learned to be an effective communicator both with your dog and other humans. You've let go of your excuses and found creative solutions to your problems. Your commitment and consistency will surely be tested, but you know exactly how to find them again after any setback. Now all that's left for you to do is *go live a great life*!

2.7 million cats and dogs in shelters are euthanized each year. I know you love your pet, and like all of us at Dogaholics, you would love to see this number go down. Now that you've made so many strides in your dog's life, I challenge you to encourage others to commit to being a better pet parent. You've seen how simple these changes can be. It's these simple changes that can and will save lives.

I'm honored to have gone on this journey with you, and I can't wait to hear about the changes you make and the life you get to lead.

I'd love for you to share your story with me! Share your before and after pictures, videos, and stories. Introduce me to your dogs, and tell me how much fun you're having. You can find me on social media at www.facebook.com/candaceD'Agnolofans - I can't wait to connect!

Make sure you also head over to www.ultimatepetparent.com and get your free pet parent guide.

Guinness and Clover are now behaving so well. As I was thinking about writing this book, I realized that the things we're unhappy with in our lives are a result of our lack of commitment. I didn't write it to call out the wonderful people who frequent Dogaholics, but rather to call out ME!

My dogs behaving badly came down to *me being lazy*, not committing, and not making the time to work with them. They needed consistency and discipline, and I wasn't providing it.

How we are as pet parents is often reflective of how we act in a lot of other areas of our lives. It could be your health and fitness. It could be your finances, your love relationships, your career, how you handle coworkers, how you handle projects, how you handle to-dos, how you handle your life goals.

I always enjoyed my time with my pets but I wasn't making the time they required of me to ensure they were living a healthy life. When they're living a healthy life, I also reap those benefits. I used to get upset thinking of all the places I would love to take them but couldn't because I didn't trust them in certain situations. It meant I was missing out on all those great memories of them while they were missing out on experiencing the kind of life they deserve.

They are living breathing beings, and they want to learn and make us proud. When they're acting out in what we see as bad behaviors, they don't know the proper way to communicate. It's not their fault – they never took an English class and can't pick up a *Guide to Understanding Your Human* book.

Do whatever you can to bring joy into your life. It can be little things or big things, but really think about each of your commitments and whether they're working to honor you and align with your values. That's when you start to really enjoy life – and you DESERVE to enjoy life.

So go! Enjoy it! And give your dog a treat from me.

You can only keep your dog under control if you can keep *yourself* under control.

To support you in moving from enabling them to training them, I have a special gift for you!

Collect your FREE gift at
ultimatepetparent.com

Candace D'Agnolo — Visit the website to get your free give now!

Founder of Dogaholics, a retail and service business, Candace D'Agnolo has helped hundreds of thousands of dog owners make confident decisions about their pets' behavior and wellness through a curated selection of quality products, services and information. Join her today and recommit to your pet. It's great for both of you!

About the Author

In 2006, Candace D'Angnolo created and opened a retail store in Chicago called Dogaholics, Inc. Within three years, she had three locations and over 20 employees. The road to building her business was paved with intense obstacles and struggles, expansion and contraction that almost put her out of business each time, but she learned quickly how to turn any crisis into growth opportunities, bringing millions of dollars into her business, allowing her to now travel the world and live a stress free life with her canine kids.

She took her initial concept of a brick and mortar location and turned it into multiple revenue streams – retail, services, online informational products, books, merchandise and now business consulting.

Candace strategically sold her retail assets in April 2016, and kept the profitable services piece to continue to grow the Dogaholics brand.

Candace is also a board member of Chicago Canine Rescue. She has helped raise over $200,000 for shelter dogs and finding many their forever homes. Having a way to give back through her business has been one of the most rewarding experiences of her life.

Visit these sites to connect with other dogaholics, like you:
www.dogaholics.com
www.facebook.com/dogaholics
www.instagram.com/dogaholics

You can find Candace at:
www.connectwithcandace.com
www.facebook.com/dogaholicsconsulting

Ge your free gift at:
www.ultimatepetparent.com

www.ingramcontent.com/pod-product-compliance
Lightning Source LLC
Chambersburg PA
CBHW071858200326
41519CB00016B/4443